Orderly
Korea
Unification

Orderly Korea Unification

With the Guarantee of Stability in East Asia

Howard Jisoo Ryu (柳 志 秀)

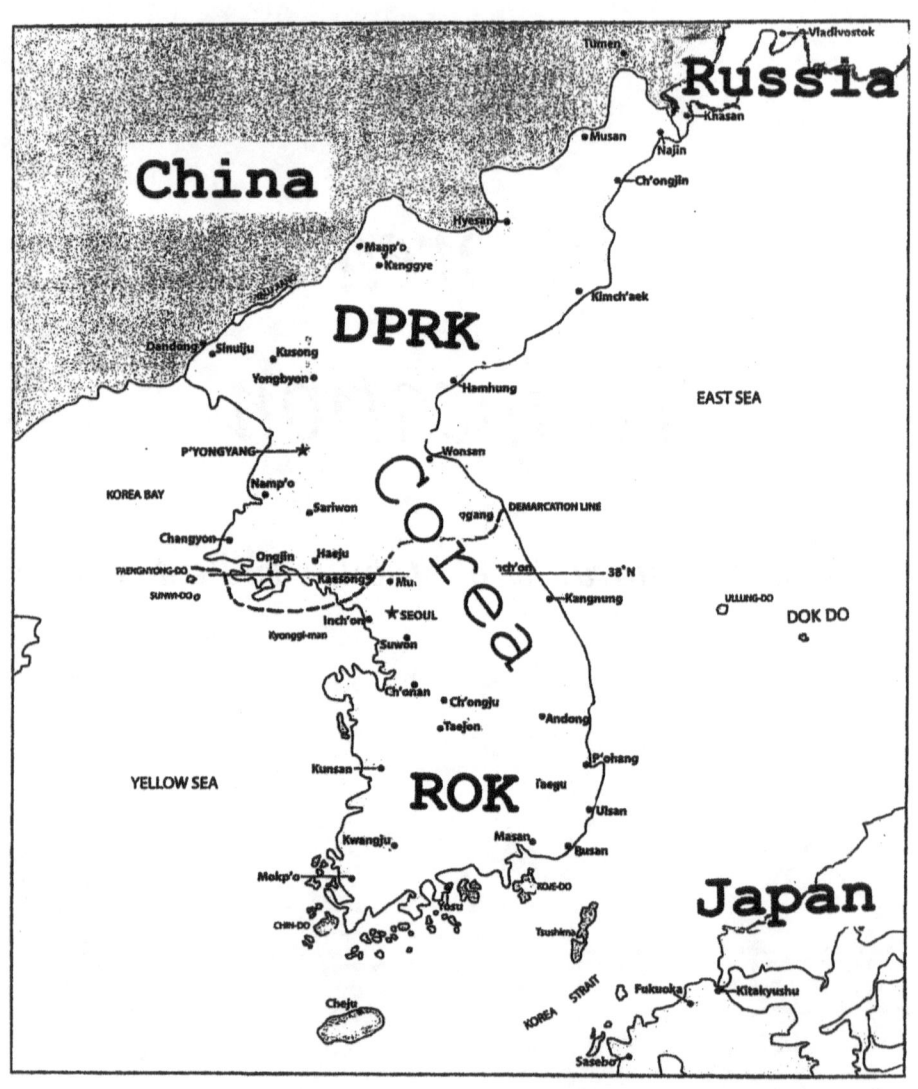

통일조선

A NEW, 2007 BLUEPRINT for:

ORDERLY

KOREA

UNIFICATION

WITH THE GUARANTEE OF STABILITY IN EAST ASIA

A BOLD, URGENT, EXTRAORDINARY, AND WIN-WIN PROPOSAL TO:

People of the South Korea (ROK),
People of the North Korea (DPRK),
Governments of China, Japan, Russia, and the USA, &
Secretary-General and General Assembly President of the United Nations
for

New ⟨ COREA ⟩ State

Library of Congress Control Number: 2007904138
ISBN: Softcover   978-1-4257-6072-4

This book was printed in the United States of America.

To order additional copies of this book, contact:
Xlibris Corporation
1-888-795-4274
www.Xlibris.com
Orders@Xlibris.com
41102

Contents

Acknowledgments 15

Preface 19

Letter to Members of the UN Exploratory Committee 25

SUMMARY AND INTRODUCTION 31

Chapter 1: TIME IS NOW TO ACT—WHY SO URGENT? 39
    1-A. GOAL 1: Rescue of North Korean Lives Dying Daily in
            Hundreds, through the Peaceful Unification 39
    1-B. GOAL 2: Stability of East Asian Region Through the
            United Nations 41

Chapter 2: CURRENT UNIFICATION SCENARIOS AND
    THEIR DRAWBACKS 43

Chapter 3: MAJOR FACTORS CONCERNING
    KOREAN PENINSULA 49
    3-A. A Story of Adoption, Not Marriage 49
    3-B. Deadlock Korean War 51
    3-C. Reconstruction and Current Vibrant Economy of the
            South Republic State 53
    3-D. Dismal Economy of North Korea 53
    3-E. Daily Deaths of North Koreans in Hundreds—
            Human Rights Abuses 55
    3-F. Kim Dynastic State and Its Valid Recognition 57
    3-G. Living Lessons to All Koreans from Iraqi Conflict—
            A Potential Korea Nightmare 59
    3-H. Security of North Korean Leaders 61

Chapter 4: KOREA UNIFICATION—
    FORMATION OF UNIFIED COREA 65
    4-A. Fundamental Elements of Unified Government 65
    4-B. Governmental Type of the Corea State 67

4-C. Prerequisites to the Orderly Unification Process.................. 71

4-D. Funds Required for Unification and Savings by
       DCM Unification Process Over Other Processes 73

4-E. Benefits from the Immediate Korea Unification 79

**Chapter 5: STABILITY OF EAST ASIA THROUGH
THE UNITED NATIONS...83**

5-A. The Guarantee by the United Nations to the
       Unified Corea.. 85

5-B. The Guarantee by the Unified Corea to the
       United Nations 91

Chapter 6: RECONCILATION MESSAGES IN CONCLUSION 97

6-A. Message to the People of South Korea 97

6-B. Message to the People of North Korea.................................. 99

6-C. Message to the Neighboring Countries: China, Japan,
       Russia, and the United States... 99

6-D. Message to the Secretary General Ban Ki-moon and
       the General Assembly President Sheikha Haya
       Rashed Al Khalifa of the United Nations 103

References... 109

List of Figures 113

Figure 1. Current economic situation of six nations
           concerning the Korean peninsula,
           taken from Table 1, updated on March 15, 2007 115

Figure 2. The chronological view of the history on the
           peninsula until the formation of the two
           separate states on the peninsula 117

Figure 3. DPRK and ROK were born by adoption process
           when the Cold War began between two
           superpowers; USSR and USA.. 119

Figure 4. This figure shows the current situation of the
           DPRK and the ROK, the proposed unified
           Government in retrospect, and the results
           of the unification process... 121

Figure 5. The summary of Chapter 5 providing the
            United Nations with two-way guarantee of the
            stability in East Asia.. 123

List of Tables **125**
    Table 1. Comparative Facts of 6 Nations: S. Korea, N. Korea,
        China, Japan, Russia, and the United States 127
    Table 2. Unification Capital Cost 131
    Table 3. Comparison of Unified Corea with two
        Current Koreas 133

List of Appendices **135**

Appendix 1: History of Korea for the last 2000 years **137**
    A. Description of the Korean Peninsula 137
    B. Origin of the Korean People 139
    C. A Brief History of Korea up to the Fourteenth Century 139
    D. Korean History for the Last 500 Years 139

Appendix 2: Founders of Korea Kingdoms or States **145**
    A. General Wang Geon (877-943)—
       Taejo of Goryeo (936-943) 145
    B. General Yi Seong Gye (Lee Sung-Gye;1335-1408)—Taejo of
       Chosun(1392-1398) also known as Yi Chosun Dynasty 147
    C. General Kim Il Sung (1912-1994)—President of
       North Korea (DPRK) (1972-1994) 151
    D. Dr. Rhee Syng Man (1875-1965)—President of South Korea
       (ROK)(1948-1960) 155

Biographical Record of Jisoo Ryu, Author **161**

Dedicated to my late parents, loving father Heonyeol Ryu and glorious mother Oksoon Shim.

This monograph is *dedicated* to North Koreans who have died or who are suffering due to the human rights abuses committed by the regime of North Korea. In spite of economic hardship, the regime has built up unimaginable military strength, including a nuclear arsenal. Such a military build-up has been designed to meet the challenging threat of the most powerful country in the world—America, particularly after the end of the Cold War in the 1990s. The persistence of US forces in the South has perpetuated the North Korean regime so that the human rights abuses have become necessary components for its own bare survival. Now is the time for the world to realize this inhumane situation and to rectify it, as proposed here.

Peace be with the world.

A humble *admiration* goes to Albert Einstein's fascination on Spinoza's pantheism. Professor Einstein found the most powerful, scientific formulas on the basis of exceptional logics. Many of them unlocked the mysteries of our marvelously arranged universe. Later they were rightly verified by numerous, actual experiments.

In this monograph, a bold, urgent, extraordinary and win-win formula is presented on the basis of the exceptional interpretation of historical facts. This tiny formula is the new, 2007 blueprint for an *orderly and immediate* Korea unification with the guarantee of stability in East Asia. As great trees can sprout from tiny seeds and beautiful minds can be born from tiny eggs, a giant contribution to the world peace will start from this tiny formula. Let us all together prove this tiny idea to be a real winner by applying it to such a difficult problem of the Korean peninsula.

A Plea For Human Society To Come Together/Unite.

Acknowledgments

Throughout my career, I have basically been a researcher, seeking solutions to difficult problems on a variety of topics. During the latter part of my trained, professional life as an exploration geophysicist, I engaged in exploring for hydrocarbon deposits through difficult rocks under deep water. My work was successful in seismically seeing through those rocks down to useful targets one to three miles deep from the water bottom. More than ten years after I retired, it has been reported that the latest discovery in that deep water area contains more than half of the known quantity in the lower 48 states of the USA. This discovery is a direct result of my early involvement as a principal researcher. In numerous cases, the various research results from different angles produce unimaginable conclusions.

Since my retirement in 2005, I have spent the last two years in researching the Korean unification. My goal is to find a reasonable way of achieving the orderly and peaceful unification as early as possible, so we can urgently save North Korean lives dying daily in the hundreds due to the human rights abuses committed by the regime of North Korea. It is ironic to find that these abuses have become necessary components for the regime's own survival, in light of geopolitical relations among the nations surrounding the peninsula. In spite of grave difficulties to this problem, I think I have found the unique and comprehensive solution from my research through Korean history and contemporary engagements of the nations.

The solution is historically viable, immediately applicable and financially profitable. It has two elements in its process—orderly Korean unification

and the guarantee of stability in East Asia, both being in theory. Theory would not be of any value, unless applied. Professor Albert Einstein found the most powerful, theoretical formulas on the basis of exceptional logics. Many of them unlocked the mysteries of the marvelously arranged universe. Later the formulas were rightly verified by their practical applications. The solution presented in this monograph is bold, urgent, extraordinary in nature, and a win-win formula that is strictly based on the exceptional interpretation of historical facts. Let us as a human race attempt to prove this for its value and validity.

The information contained herein is of general historical knowledge and can be supported by public source books, encyclopedias and various websites. I believe the information is considered factual. It is my regret that numerous, previous researchers in this field have not been acknowledged properly in this monograph, mainly because of its urgency in completion before printing.

The manuscript has been proofread by Sabina Peterson and Sara Ryu, and further improved by publisher. As a result, its readability was significantly enhanced. I sincerely appreciate their kind assistance. In this monograph, Korea unification, Korean unification and Korean reunification are synonymously used. The cover art and the images for the interior were taken from the book titled "A Survey of Korean Dance" by Kim Jung Yeon (1971).

In closing, I would like to mention a couple of personal issues. My permanent domicile at birth is Chung Cheong Do in South Korea and my birth place is Hamhung City in North Korea. I was raised in South Korea from the age of four before arriving in the USA at the age of 22. The first point is that I am not a communist, nor a communist-sympathizer, nor an admirer of Kim Il Sung, Kim Jong Il or Rhee Syng Man, but I am a fair-minded person looking at things in an objective manner. Secondly, I hope readers understand that the subject matter is a difficult one to cover from all angles. In the monograph, there may be some points which are missed, hard to understand, difficult to swallow, or incorrect in the English usage, etc. Also, since some readers are new to Korea, I tried my best to explain things as clear as possible within each subchapter in a self-contained manner, so that repetitions may have been occurred. I extend my apologies in advance and appreciate your support and understanding.

Finally, readers can direct any question to me via email or challenge me regarding issues relating to the theoretical concepts presented in this monograph. I will be more than happy to defend them.

Peace be with us!

Peace Be With the World !
A Plea for Human Society To Come Together/Unite !

Preface

The division of the Korean peninsula was an unfortunate product of the Cold War created by two superpowers which emerged in conjunction with World War II: the Soviet Union leading the Communist blocs and the United States of America leading the pro-western nations. The most likely alternative to this division would have been a unified Communist state. This alternative would also have been a reality if the US did not defend South Korea during the Korean War, in which the United States directly fought China. In this regard, there is no doubt that all South Koreans, including the author, sincerely appreciate the assistance and sacrifice made by the Americans during the Korean War and thereafter, regardless of whether they were made for their own life-or-death struggle against the Soviet Union or the mere survival of South Korea.

The presence of the US forces in South Korea and Japan during the last 50+ years has produced several obvious results, although quite differently in the South than in the North of the peninsula. Now a military free-rider, South Korea has not invested in the military, but rather has focused on economic development and is today the 13th economic power and a member of the trillion GDP club in the world. Meanwhile, North Korea has continually felt so threatened by the most powerful country in the world-America that it has been able to invest only in the military, including the nuclear arsenal. Particularly after the collapse of the Soviet Blocs in the 1990s, the North became isolated and unable to make any advance in its economic front. The result is that the survival of North Korea as a state is currently at risk and the collapse of the North Korean regime

has been anticipated by experts every year. Moreover, the South is well positioned to defend itself. It possesses more than 30 times the economic strength in terms of GDP and twice the population of the North. It has a vast technological lead and has stolen away the North's allies, as well as the friendship of most other states. Thus, the economic miracle of the South was achievable under the protection of the US defense system, whereas the dismal economy of the North is a result of the continual presence of the US forces in the South and the collapse of the Soviet Blocs.

In light of these economic developments, now is the perfect time for the government of South Korea to make a bold and immediate move towards an ORDERLY and peaceful Korean unification with the guarantee of stability in East Asia by the help of the United Nations. It is regrettable to say that the Government of North Korea must give up the idea of unifying the Korean peninsula on its own terms and accept the unification mode, proposed here, in exchange for the future securities of the North Korean leaders and their descendants. If they do so, severe human tolls and destructive chaos during the unification process will be avoided—unlike the current situation in Iraq. This monograph reveals the outline of the unification mode in a skeleton form which should be satisfactory to the majority of the Korean people and to the demands of other nations concerning the peninsula. It has numerous benefits, as explained in this report, with a couple of drawbacks. Most important is the end of the human rights abuses by the North Korean regime. Also equally importantly, this new, 2007 unification scenario turns out to save more than $100 Billion in unification capital cost, in comparison with other known unification scenarios.

The basic principle of the proposal is that the Korean problem on the Korean peninsula must and can be solved only by the initiation of Koreans themselves. What is more, the time is ripe for this situation to be addressed. Today the two Koreas have become at best a peripheral security interest to America, while economic relations have been warming up for mutual prosperity among the powerful neighboring countries—China, Japan, Russia and the US, particularly after the end of the Cold War. Their governments must unselfishly support this new unification endeavor of the Koreans, for themselves and by themselves in the 21st century, along with the guarantee of stability in East Asia through the United Nations. The Korea unification, outlined in this proposal, will provide peace, prosperity and no further nuclear threat by North Korea to all nations in the world. Of course, there will initially be temporary disturbances across the peninsula during the unification process. Those will be local matters and temporary in nature. Furthermore, the Koreans are socially and intellectually conformed

enough to resolve those matters in a reasonable fashion under the rules of law of the new COREA** state.

A liberty is taken to request the Secretary-General Ban Ki Moon and the General Assembly President Sheikha Haya Rashed Al Khalifa of the United Nations to immediately initiate the formation of a UN Exploratory Committee(UNEC) for conducting a feasibility study on the proposal outlined in this report. The letter to the members of the UNEC follows in the next. As shown in the letter, the UNEC is suggested to consist of 11 members of the United Nations for embarking on this giant step towards the Korean unification, thereby leading to a safer world. Time is of essence to end the human rights abuses and to save the lives dying daily in the hundreds in North Korea.

Howard Jisoo Ryu, Author of the Proposal
Citizen of the United Nations
Citizen of the United States of America
Formerly Citizen of the South Korea

May 2007

** The early western history shows that the current Korean peninsula was introduced to the western world as Corea before the 20th century. It is also believed that C of Corea was changed to K during the Japanese colonial period (1910-1945). In this report, the unified state is to be called as Corea, which is also believed to be originated from the Goryeo Kingdom (936-1392) over the peninsula (See Appendix 1 or Figure 2). This means that the effect of the Japanese colony still remains over the peninsula until the new Corea is formed as a unified state over the peninsula.

Letter to: Members of the UN Exploratory Committee (UNEC)

Representative of the United Nations, Chairperson,
Representative of Norway, Vice Chairperson,
Representative of India, Vice Chairperson,
Representative of German, Unification Process Advisor,
Representative of Singapore, Unification Process Advisor,
Representative of South Korea, Project Manager,
Representative of North Korea, Deputy Manager,
Representative of China, Unification Fund Advisor,
Representative of Japan, Unification Fund Advisor,
Representative of Russia, Project Advisor, and
Representative of the United States, Project Advisor.

It is here suggested that the UNEC consists of the 11 members listed above. However, the Chairperson should replace some members, if appropriate.

The proposal, outlined in a skeleton form in this report, is to unify the two Koreas into one Corea state and to have two non-aggression agreements signed by four powerful countries—China, Japan, Russia and the United States plus Corea, for the stability of the East Asian region. These two goals of the proposal should be exceptionally viable, practically doable and reasonably acceptable to the people of the South Korea, the North Korea

and the United Nations. They are described in detail in Chapters 4 and 5 of this report on the basis of the historical and current factors involving the Korean peninsula as discussed in Chapter 3. Once the two goals are achieved, the new Corea state will possess the following basic elements;

   a. The entire social, political, economic and governmental systems of the current democracy in South Korea to be applied across the entire Korean peninsula,

   b. Total removal of human rights abuses from the entire peninsula,

   c. Future guaranteed securities of North Korean leaders and their descendants, and, in exchange, their full cooperation for the unification process,

   d. Minimal capital cost for the unification, meaning a large saving more than $100 Billion in comparison with the capital cost estimates for other unification scenarios,

   e. Stability of the East Asian region through the United Nations,

   f. All of the WMD possibly existing in North Korea put under the United Nations' supervision, and

   g. No loss of any one nation's influence over the peninsula.

Then, after the unification, all citizens of the new Corea state will enjoy the freedom and liberty currently enjoyed by the citizens of South Korea, under the rules of law of the new state.

The mission of the UNEC is threefold.

1. Each one of the 11 UNEC members is to understand the proposal outlined in this report, clearly and unquestionably. For this step, the author of the proposal is available to present the details of the proposed items in person or via phone or email to the UNEC members, individually or collectively.

2. The members of the UNEC are to carry out their feasibility studies on the proposed items, in consultation with appropriate governmental agencies of the nations involved.

3. Upon the completion of their feasibility studies, the Chairperson will call a final meeting where the UNEC's recommendation is to be made. If the recommendation is positive, the UNEC is to produce a road map toward the successful completion of the proposed items. If the recommendation becomes negative or needs modifications on the proposal, the UNEC's final report is written in that effect.

Time is of essence here to save the lives dying daily in North Korea, due to the human rights abuses by the regime of the North Korea. We, the UNEC members, will meet the first official meeting on the designated date.

Respectfully,

Chairperson Designated
Representative of the United Nations
May 2007

Summary and Introduction

Each day the North Koreans are dying in hundreds at 10 prison camps, by starvation, and in mountainous areas within Chinese territory just across the border from North Korea. The rescue of these people dying daily is the most urgent, humanitarian mission, which must be addressed immediately by South Koreans as well as North Koreans, and further by the people of all nations in the United Nations. The rescue of these people dying daily can be achieved only by the orderly and immediate unification of the two Koreas existing in the Korean peninsula, which in turn requires the stability of the East Asian region guaranteed to the nations under discussion. A bold, extraordinary, and win-win solution to this difficult problem has been found, which is based on the exceptional interpretation of Korean history, and is to be supported by the help of the United Nations. Chapter 1 describes the goals of this study. In relation to these goals, the current, widely visualized unification scenarios and their drawbacks are discussed in Chapter 2.

The solution in this report has not been recorded elsewhere to the knowledge of the author, but it is immediately applicable, and, also importantly, will save more than $100 Billion in capital cost for the unification of the two Koreas in comparison with those of other known approaches. The capital cost is meant to be the cost for doubling the GDP of North Korea in a short period (4 to 5 years), immediately after the unification, as defined in the book (1) written by Charles Wolf and Kamil Akramov of Rand Corporation (2005) (titled "North Korean Paradoxes"). The non-capital portion of the unification cost is too uncertain to be analyzed but can be projected as in the range of $100 Billion.

Korean unification is tied to numerous issues. The main issues at the center of the solution are as follows;

1. The entire social, political, economic and governmental systems of the current democracy in South Korea to be applied across the entire Korean peninsula after the unification, mainly because the North Korean state barely exists, given the extremely poor condition of its economic life line (See Figure 1 and Table 1),
2. Total removal of human rights abuses from the entire peninsula,
3. Future guaranteed security of North Korean leaders and their descendants, and, in exchange, their full cooperation for the unification process,
4. Comparatively minimal capital cost for unification,
5. Stability of the East Asian region through the support of the United Nations,
6. All of the WMD possibly existing in North Korea to be put under the United Nations' supervision, and
7. No loss of the influence of any one nation over the peninsula through the unification process, as proposed here.

The results of our research have found only one approach of satisfactorily achieving all of the seven issues above. Our approach is essentially on the basis of Korean history. Thus, readers must first fully understand the major factors concerning the Korean peninsula in Chapter 3, before appreciating the merits of the proposed unification process shown in Chapter 4 and the guarantee of stability in East Asia, which is depicted in a basic framework in Chapter 5.

The proposed governmental form as detailed in Chapter 4 will provide the North Korean leaders and their descendants with their future securities, who will, in exchange, cooperatively assist the new Corea state for the *orderly* unification of the two Korea states. Unlike the current, chaotic situation in Iraq, the problems of the new Corea state will be manageable and resolvable in the spirit of cooperation among all citizens of the new state. As shown in Subchapter 4-C discussing the unification funds, the cooperative *order* of the unification process results in reducing **the unification capital cost by more than $100 Billion**, possibly more than $200 Billion, as shown in Table 2. This saving is huge in comparison with the possible cost required for the securities of the North Korean leaders and their descendants.

Chapter 5 presents the ways of how to guarantee the *stability* of the East Asian region by two non-aggression agreements through the United Nations, in order for the unification process to move forward to a successful conclusion. Then there will no longer be national or international animosity

over the Korean peninsula. As implied by the current ties of the South Korea with China, Japan, Russia and the USA, the new state of Corea will basically continue current ROK relations with these nations. Furthermore, all of the WMD possibly existing in North Korea will come under the supervision of the United Nations. In this way, there will not be any more agonizing moment at the six-party talks, which will instead have a positive resolution. Also, as the worldwide conciliatory atmosphere warms after the Cold War era and as the four major regional powers come to increasingly desire the stability of the region, it seems very timely to request them to agree on the proposed, non-aggression agreement through the United Nations, as outlined in Chapter 5.

Finally, the major task will be to make this case attractively convincing to the people of South Korea, North Korea and the nations concerned with the Korean peninsula. On the basis of eight major factors discussed in Chapter 3, the new approach of this proposal detailed in Chapters 4 and 5 will be successful and feasible only by realizing the five factual elements related to the proposed approach;

1. The governmental form of the unified Corea state is totally based on and justified from the key elements of Korea history within the last 2000 years.

2. Most world economic experts recognize that the current regime of North Korea is basically functioning on a sort of "life-support" system in light of its dismal economic performance as a nation for the last decade, as indicated in Figure 1 and Table 1. It is time that the North Korean leaders give up their will of unifying the Korean peninsula on their own terms alone and submit their political powers to the genuine formation of the new Corea state as outlined in a skeleton form in Chapter 4. In exchange for this, they and their descendants will receive a guarantee for their future security. Also, they will have significant tasks to perform for the orderly unification process during the initial transition period.

3. All citizens of the South Korea must accept the new concept on the governmental form of the new Corea state, in which the securities of the North Korean leaders and their descendants are guaranteed. It is also recognized that that security guarantee would make the Korean unification ORDERLY and that order would result in the reduction of unification capital costs by more than $100 Billion, as explained in Table 2. For a successful and orderly unification, all South Koreans must embrace their Northern brothers and sisters with open arms, leaving behind personal greed and anti-Communist feeling. It is time for the South Korean government to make a move

towards the peace of the Korean peninsula as well as the world. In this way, the North Koreans dying daily will be saved when the unification process starts.

4. The peace and stability of the East Asian region will be beneficial to all nations concerning the Korean peninsula, particularly China, Japan, Russia and the USA. It is particularly important that these four powers admit their past, unreasonable behavior, and ideologically support the concept of this proposal and financially assist the actual Korea unification process. It is also safe to say that they will recover in the long run far more than what they initially invest.

5. Secretary-General Ban and General Assembly President Al Khalifa of the United Nations must endorse this proposal regarding the human rights issues in North Korea and make their immediate resolutions to help all citizens of the new Corea state to attain their freedom and liberty they deserve.

Peace and prosperity in this region will immensely contribute to peace and prosperity throughout the world. By doing so, the wealth of the new Corea state will also be immensely increased from those of the two separate states, as shown in Table 3 and will be delightfully enjoyed freely and equally by all citizens of the peninsula.

Peace Be With the World !
A Plea for Human Society To Come Together/Unite !

Chapter 1

TIME IS NOW TO ACT—WHY SO URGENT?

The time has come for the Korean problem to be resolved by Koreans without foreign interference. Consequently, it is the time for Koreans to initiate and act in order to achieve IMMEDIATELY the two GOALS as specified below. The ultimate goal of this urgent, bold, extraordinary, and win-win proposal is to satisfy the needs of all concerned parties with the resultant Korea unification and a new peace of higher quality in the East Asian region. The urgency is critical to save human lives, as stated in Goal 1.

1-A. GOAL 1: Rescue of North Korean Lives Dying Daily in Hundreds, through the Peaceful Unification

Both South Korea and North Korea must immediately and urgently save the lives of North Koreans dying in hundreds everyday in prison camps in the North, in the Chinese border area, or by starvation, rather than wait for the collapse of the North Korean government by imploding or exploding. For this grand, humanitarian purpose, Koreans of both countries must bite the bullet and put down their own personal greed, and move forward toward immediate Korea unification, as described in Chapter 4. Let us save as many lives of our sisters and brothers, as possible, who are the citizens of our world.

Koreans must request possible assistance from the United Nations for the guaranteed stability of East Asia, making the Korean Peninsula be free of foreign forces. In this way, the concerned countries of the United Nations will be satisfied with the stability of the East Asia region, guaranteed by agreements to be newly signed under the framework of the United Nations, as stated in Goal 2.

1-B. GOAL 2: Stability of East Asian Region Through the United Nations

The United Nations must achieve the stability of East Asia through peaceful agreements among UN member nations of concern, rather than unacceptably victimizing the people living in the Korean Peninsula by military forces. In exchange from the unified Korea (called "Corea" hereafter), the United Nations is to attain a guarantee that the nuclear materials existing in the Korean Peninsula and other related weapons, if any, are to be confined under the international supervision only within the Korean Peninsula.

Koreans must act boldly to tackle this extraordinary problem of Korea unification facing all Koreans worldwide now. Most importantly, each Korean must make her or his unconditional surrender to sincere conscience on the early savings of the lives of North Korean sisters and brothers dying daily in hundreds.

Wolf and Akramov (1) of Rand Corporation, USA published in 2005 their important work on "North Korean Paradoxes: Circumstances, Costs, and Consequences of Korean Unification". They presented three scenarios for the Korea unification, which are most contemporary and well known. The three scenarios will be discussed first in the next Chapter and the new proposal is presented in Chapter 4. Each Chapter is extended separately in a self-contained form.

Chapter 2

CURRENT UNIFICATION SCENARIOS
AND THEIR DRAWBACKS

Three unification scenarios was recently discussed and analytically evaluated for unification cost by Wolf and Akramov (1) of Rand Corporation, a US think-tank, research organization in 2005. They are as follows:

Scenario A: Unification Through System Evolution and Integration

North Korea may introduce China's remarkably successful economic model, meaning that its economic system be liberated and decentralized, and the country be open to the world. The current system of Kim Jong Il's dynastic state would most unlikely permit China's model, however, and is trying to minimally increase trade with the South Korea and a few other countries. The current GDP of the North Korea is less than 4% of the South Korea, as shown in Table 1. Because of this dismal economic picture, the fate of the North Korea as a nation is at risk. Also, if happened in this mode, it would take many years to emerge and catch up to its counterpart, South Korea, therefore this mode would not meet the two goals stated above.

Scenario B: Unification Through Collapse and Absorption

As shown year after year, the North Korean regime has shown an extraordinary capacity to withstand severe internal economic adversity. The regime has been surviving basically with economic rents and other foreign aid from external sources, mostly being from China, South Korea and the United States. The regime may continue for a while, unlike East Germany which was collapsed in 1990 and absorbed by West Germany.

The question is how many North Koreans will die in the interim. Bennet(2) presented several excellent view points in his commentary.

— President Bush named three regimes in the axis of evil in 2002; Iraq, Iran and North Korea. The Iraqi regime change created many unexpected and costly problems. The time to begin preparing for these problems in the Korean peninsula is NOW.
— Like a collapsing skyscraper, a collapsing North Korean regime could cause a lot of damage to everything surrounding it.
— Kim Jong Il is well aware of the damage his fall could cause and the fear this generates. There is a probability that a post-Kim North Korea would be even more dangerous than North Korea is today.
— Kim may make his final act of nuclear attack on neighbors, killing hundreds of thousands of people or more.

This mode may also take too many human tolls to be acceptable and it does not meet the two goals mentioned above.

Scenario C. Unification Through Conflict Generated by Provocation

Conflict between North and South Korean can arise through several possible events that can be precipitated by provoked or unprovoked actions of the North, the South or the United States. It seems that China would not allow such a military conflict. If it did, the unification would be more costly in human lives and material damages, so that this mode would not be acceptable.

All of the scenarios above cannot achieve the two goals set out earlier in this proposal. The key of the current proposal in Chapter 4 is to achieve the Korea unification immediately in an orderly manner. The necessary order would be gained only by the assistance of Kim Jong Il himself, his military machine and North Korean Officials, unlike the current situation of Iraqi conflict. This means that Korea unification must be achieved by Koreans alone without any external intervention by foreign nations.

In the next section, the current situation of the North and South Korea is presented, mostly taken from public internet websites. The validity of the data shown may be questioned, but may not be too remote from their truth to discredit them. Based on this data, the new proposal described in Chapters 4 and 5 would only be successful when each party concerned is to perform its part toward the primary goals set out earlier. The actions of each party are achievable and justified by the data and the history of the Korean peninsula. They are described as messages in Chapter 6.

Peace Be With the World !
A Plea for Human Society To Come Together/Unite !

Chapter 3

MAJOR FACTORS CONCERNING
KOREAN PENINSULA

Each party in this peace process must reconcile possibly unacceptable issues, uniquely to each individual or country, in order for these grand goals of the peaceful Korea unification and the overall regional peace to be successful. There are possibly eight current, important issues, concerning the unification process, each of which is examined in an objective manner and must be fully understood to accept the proposed structure of the new government.

3-A. A Story of Adoption, Not Marriage

In August 1945 when Japan made her unconditional surrender to US forces for the end of WWII, there were two child orphan brothers, called here NK(North Korea) and SK (South Korea), returning to the Korean peninsula, whose parents were killed during the Japanese colonial period which lasted 36 years. Appendix 1 depicts the history of the Korean peninsula in a cursory manner leading to this modern period, along with brief descriptions of Korean peninsula and people. Also, Figure 2 shows the chronological view of the history with an emphasis on the founders of kingdoms and states from Goryeo dynasty. The victorious US regime separated these two brothers by the 38th parallel line in between NK in the

North Korea and SK in the South Korea. NK was adopted by the USSR and became a Communist state, whereas the US adopted SK, who became molded into a western-style household. These two brothers were growing up under their protected houses, respectively happy, during the Cold War period. This early situation is depicted in Figure 3.

Since 1991 when the Soviets' Communism collapsed and Russia started, NK has received little assistance from Russia and the eastern Communist states, resulting in even food shortage, whereas SK grew strongly and became economically vibrant under US protection. NK became very difficult in maintaining its own internal, living affairs, particularly by the continuing, ideological and invasive threat of the US regime. More than sixty years after these adoptions, now is the time in which the grownup man SK comes out of the unnecessary protection of his adopted parent, the US, in order to help his brother NK solve in the very least his hunger problem, and all adopted parents must stay away from these brothers. If SK comes out of the direct influence of the US, that is not meant to be a friendly divorce between SK and the US, but an independent move of SK still amicable with, but physically separated from the US. SK and the US were never married, but one was adopted by the other in 1945. Both will benefit and be profitable trade partners once separated. Moreover, it is unfathomable to describe how miserable NK's (North Korea) economic situation is and how urgently NK needs SK's assistance for better mutual survival together in this competitive world of the 21st century.

3-B. Deadlock Korean War

With Stalin's approval at the onset of the Cold War, Kim Il Sung of North Korea attacked South Korea on June 25, 1950 and the war stopped with a truce on July 27, 1953. Kim Il Sung made a bitter assessment in the summer of 1950 (Eberstadt, 7):

> "Had it not been for the direct military intervention of the US imperialists, we could have reunified our fatherland and completely liberated the people in the southern half from the police state tyranny of the US imperialists and the Syngman Rhee clique".

The casualties of both sides involving the two Koreas, China, US and other countries, were huge. Lee (8) reported in 2007 the current estimates of the war casualties include 37,904 US soldiers, 4,521 other UN forces, 103,248 S. Koreans, 316,579 N. Koreans and 422,612 Chinese soldiers, and the destruction of more than 30% of all houses in the Korean peninsula,

mostly done by the bombing operations of the US Air Force. Were such causalities and destruction necessary to win the war? It can be viewed that such might have been necessary at the onset of the Cold War between two super powers. Now 50 years later, the Cold War ended, the US remains the only super power, and both parties still are in enemy relations. It is time for other nations to let Korea achieve eternal peace. It is also time for all Koreans to put miserable memories of the Korean War behind an unfortunate and brief chapter of the Korean history of 4000 years.

3-C. Reconstruction and Current Vibrant Economy of the South Republic state:

In 1950, every Korean in the South was content to not be under the Communist North Korean regime, and highly appreciated the assistance from the free western nations during the Korean War, which was a civil war. Most of the South Koreans are still very thankful particularly to citizens of the US and its government which has been providing the ROK (South Korea) with the necessary security for reconstruction and economic development. Now the South Korea has become so economically strong, it is the 13th economic power Republic state in the world whose sovereignty is based solely on popular consent, representation and control under the rule of law. It is time that the ROK stands on her own without losing her steam in the world market, together with North Korea, to become the unified Corea. This means that the ROK can walk out from the US umbrella as a grownup state, not making an amiable divorce with the US (see Chapter 3-A), but becoming a friendly and equal partner to every nation in the world.

It is historically important to call the unified state Corea. Before the Japanese colonized the Korean peninsula in 1910, the peninsula was known in the western world as Corea or Chosun, as recorded in the western written documentations. It was unfortunate that the Japanese made the peninsula known to the world as Korean peninsula. Now is time the new state is called Corea once unified, as proposed here.

3-D. Dismal Economy of North Korea

Table 1 compares facts on South Korea (SK), North Korea (NK), China, Japan, Russia and USA in terms of 25 categories. This data was taken from the Factbook of CIA of the US, updated on March 15, 2007. In this table, the most striking categories are under the economic comparison. The GDP (Gross Domestic Product) by purchasing power parity of North Korea is about 3.39% of South Korea, 0.40% of China, 0.95% of Japan, 2.31% of

Russia, and 0.31% of the US, and the GDP per capita of North Korea is about 7.44% of South Korea, 23.7% of China, 5.44% of Japan, 14.9% of Russia and 4.14% of the US, as indicated in Figure 1. The total export of North Korea is estimated to be $1.34 Billion whereas that of South Korea is $326 Billion. The oil consumption of North Korea in 2004 was estimated to be 25,000 bbl/day(1.16% of SK) and that of South Korea is 2,149,000 bbl/day. These representative statistics mean that North Korean economy is extremely weak such that it cannot be sustainable for too long before the country's economy collapses.

Despite its small population (47% of South Korea) and dismal budget, North Korea is heavily militarized, claiming to have an army of more than one million soldiers, as well as claiming development of nuclear weapons and long-range missiles. It also maintains rows of massive artillery batteries designed to inflict heavy casualties on South Korea in the event of international conflict. For the sake of discussion, let us assume North Korea's budget of $20 Billion for the fiscal year 2005 and its military spending to be 30% of the budget at most. Then, its military expenditure is about $6 Billion, whereas that of South Korea is more than $30 Billion with an army less than half of North Korea's (see Table 1). Regardless of respective military expenditures, both parties are now to spend their resources not on military purposes, but on modernizing North Korea into the 21st century.

3-E. Daily Deaths of North Koreans in Hundreds— Human Rights Abuses

The North Korea government is essentially a dictatorship—previously operated by Kim Il Sung, and now by his son Kim Jong Il, in a form of a personality cult. The government enforces loyalty and obedience through its Ministry of People's Security, which requires citizens to spy on each other, including family members. As Head (3) described, the government divided its citizens into three castes based on their perceived loyalty to the Dear Leader Kim: core, wavering and hostile. Most of the wealth is concentrated within the core group (estimated to be about 25%) including military personnel, technocrats, and top echelons of the Korean Workers Party, while the hostile group (about 30%) is denied employment and subject to starvation, including all members of minority faiths, as well as descendants of perceived enemies of the state. The 30 % of the total population, 23 million, in the hostile group comes to be approximately 8 million people. Many of these people will die daily by starvation and without normal living conditions. One hundredth of 1% of 8 million people in trouble is 800. These people need to be urgently rescued.

The North Korea government has no legal system with due process. It imprisons, tortures and executes prisoners at will, and maintains 10 concentration camps, with a total of between 200,000 and 250,000 prisoners contained therein, as reported by Head (3). Conditions in the camps are so terrible that the annual casualty rate has been estimated to be as high as 25%, meaning that more than a minimum of 50,000 prisoners a year or 140 a day die in these camps. Koreans, both from the South and the North, must work together to stop these inhumane deaths.

Between 50,000 and 300,000 North Koreans has been reported to seek refuge in China from starvation and political persecution in North Korea every year. China has rounded an increased amount of North Korean defectors as more sneaked across its border to seek sustenance since the mid-1990s after the end of the Cold War. China regards them as illegal economic migrants rather than refuges and repatriates some of them back to the North. Once returned, defectors face harsh punishment. Many of these refugees remaining in China are hiding in North Eastern China, commonly estimated to be 100,000 to 300,000 by international NGOs (see Refugees International (4)). Some of them reach welcoming South Korea through a third country, but their paths have not been so easy that a part of them dies.

The perils discussed above are confronting many individual North Koreans daily. The exact number of the daily deaths resulting from these perils is hard to be estimated, even roughly, but it can be projected that the minimum is possibly 500 North Koreans dying daily under the harsh, economic or political conditions of one type or another, as discussed above. Both the South and the North must work together to save these lives through an immediate and orderly, peaceful unification proposed in Chapter 4. The unification process must be orderly and peaceful without incurring any further, unnecessary human cost. This order and peacefulness can be attained only with the help of Kim Jong Il, the current head of the North Korea, whose governmental nature is discussed in the next subchapter.

3-F. Kim Dynastic State and Its Valid Recognition

Starting from the dawn of the first century in Korean history, the kings of three kingdoms, called Gogurye, Baekje and Silla, ruled the Korean peninsula and the vast southern portion of Manchuria (See Appendix 1). When Silla unfied these kingdoms with help of the Chinese Ming dynasty in the seventh century, the large portion of the land beyond the parallel line above present Pyongyang was lost. The current boundary of the Korean peninsula was recaptured when Goryeo dynasty was founded in 936 after the unified Silla was submitted to Goryeo. Since that time, the Korean peninsula was ruled by successive kings, like other kingdoms in the world,

until Korea was colonized by Japan in 1910, when Emperor Soonjong of Yi Chosun dynasty was dethroned by force.

Essentially the Korean history of last 2000 years recognizes four well-known founders of new kingdoms or states over the Korean peninsula. They are General Wang Geon of Goryeo dynasty begun in 936, General Yi Seong Gye of Yi Chosun dynasty founded in 1392, General Kim Il Sung of North Korea, whose presidency was proclaimed in 1972, and Dr. Rhee Syng Man of South Korea, who was elected as the first president by a parliamentary vote in 1948. In Appendix 2, these founders are compared in regard to their recognized status in terms of background, mode for rise to power, legacy, and family.

Dr. Rhee appears quite different from the other three founders, particularly being a Christian scholar, rather than a military person. He was installed to be the first president of South Korea (Republic of Korea), which now is democratic and economically vibrant 60 years later. Unlike Dr. Rhee, Kim Il Sung shows a large degree of similarities to King Wang of Goryeo and founder Yi of the Yi Chosun dynasty, as discussed in Appendix 2. Kim was an anti-Japanese general in fighting for Korea independence before rising to power in the North. It appears justifiable then that such similarities prove the right qualifications of Kim Il Sung to be the founding King of the North Korean kingdom 60 years ago. In reality, Kim Il Sung passed his kingship to his son, Kim Jong Il, in 1994 to continue their kingdom in the North. This means that the Kim dynasty reigned over half of the Korean peninsula in the North as a continuation of the Yi Chosun dynasty, with an interruption of 36 years by the Japanese colonization.

All South Koreans must recognize this dynastic nature of the North Korean Regime ruled by Kim Jong Il as its current king. They must respect the King of the Northern, neighboring kingdom like any other world leader, regardless of whether the current regime is preferred or not. In this case, the Northern neighbor of South Korea is its brother in history, which needs immediate assistance from the Southern brother in order to save the lives dying daily in the North (see Subchapters 3-A and 3-E). Other US researchers also view this dynastic nature of North Korea from different angles. Martin (5) described Kim Il Sung in detail in his book titled "Under the Loving Care of the Fatherly Leader-North Korea and the Kim Dynasty" in 2004. Wolf (6) referred the North to the Kim dynastic regime in discussing about the regime's revenues in 2006.

3-G. Living Lessons to All Koreans from Iraqi Conflict— A Potential Korea Nightmare

Similarities exist between the Kim Jong Il regime and the former Saddam Hussein regime. Saddam, a dictator, had a large army, which was

disbanded after his fall, and Kim's regime has a million plus men army under his dictatorship. In Saddam's case, his dictatorship collapsed by the invasion of the US military forces in 2003. The unemployed soldiers of the disbanded Iraqi army have turned to insurgency and fighting for years against the US forces and the Iraqi police force, leading to the current sectarian war.

Let us look at a scenario in which the Kim's regime collapses suddenly without much order where the ROK has to absorb the North. Former North Korean soldiers may resort to insurgency against the capitalist South Koreans. Proliferation of nuclear or other weapons could be one of the insurgents' few options to generate income. In addition, there is a high probability that millions of refugees would flee the poverty and misery of what had been North Korea, for the prosperous South and China. These scenarios look like the beginning of a nightmare to South Koreans and people in the neighboring countries. The only feasible option to avoid such a catastrophe is to realize Korean unification over the peninsula with a reasonable degree of order. This will come only from the cooperative and genuine assistance of North Korean leaders, including Kim Jong Il himself, as next discussed.

3-H. Security of North Korean Leaders

The constitution of the DPRK (North Korea) has one overriding policy objective, which is the unconditional unification of the whole Korea under its own terms, meaning the complete victory of Socialism or Communism. This is totally unlikely to happen in light of the major current of world trend. Fundamentally, the North has underestimated the importance of economic performance for its long term prospects of unifying the peninsula on its own terms. It is apparent and must be recognized that the North Korea's policy objective of unifying the nation on its own term is not feasible, and its own survival as a separate nation is at stake because of its poor economic performance (see Subchapters 3-C and 3-D). This situation partly resulted from the half-century long threat from the currently strongest nation on this planet, America. In response to this continuing threat, the North has been building a massive army and military machine. This is not a productive element nor useful for its economic advancement. Now it seems to be an inescapable reality that North Korea can no longer take even its state survival for granted. Before the undesirable collapse of the North as discussed (see Subchapter 3-G), it is time that South Koreans should seek genuine cooperation from the North Korean leaders for the desirable orderly unification. In return to receiving their genuine cooperation, the new Corea state should provide the North Korea leaders

and their descendants with firm future securities. The security package should include ways of utilizing the large North Korean military members in replacing the crumbling infrastructures in the North.

In this way, the unification process discussed in Chapter 4 will be an orderly one. While the North Korean leaders will receive their future security, its citizens in the North will become free from the current dictator, at least under the current system. Thus, the unification will become a win-win process not only to all Koreans but also to the nations involved, once the United Nations brokers two additional agreements to be discussed in Chapter 5. This process will certainly require all Koreans to sacrifice a certain degree of self interest. The sacrificing elements will be very temporary and minimal in comparison with the benefits resulting from the orderly unification, which will certainly achieve the two goals set out at the beginning of this proposal.

Peace Be With the World !
A Plea for Human Society To Come Together/Unite !

Chapter 4

KOREA UNIFICATION—
FORMATION OF UNIFIED COREA

This report sketches the framework of proposals in a skeleton form for Korean unification and the stability of the East Asia. The detailed aspects of the processes are left to appropriate governmental officials.

4-A. Fundamental Elements of Unified Government

The two governments must be successfully combined into the unified Corea, whose system must permit the current vibrant economy of the ROK to continue and make the diminishing, dismal economy of the DPRK grow rapidly in the world market. With these basic principles, the new state must possess seven fundamental elements although there may be other constitutional elements required. These elements will satisfy the needs of both current Korean states in a two-way relationship:

1. It is here suggested that the new state is called Corea with its governmental capitol at Kaeseong (Capital of Goryeo) or Panmunjeom located between Seoul and Pyongyang. The entirely new Corea government will be built in a 21st century fashion to bring together the current governments in Seoul and Pyongyang.

2. Every citizen of Corea must have freedom and liberty currently enjoyed by the citizens of the ROK under the rules of law within the ROK constitution (see Subchapters 3-A, 3-C, and 3-E).

3. The regulations of Corea must permit the current economy of the ROK to continue with additional safeguards, in which the economy in the North grows rapidly to meet the world standard (see Subchapters 3-C and 3-D).

4. The governmental system of Corea must provide guaranteed security to Kim Jong Il and his descendants. It must also provide other North Korean leaders and their descendants with guaranteed security for a limited time period. In return, the North Korean leaders must cooperate with, and assist, the new Corea officials for the orderly unification, at least for three years from the starting date of the unification process (see Subchapters 3-F, 3-G and 3-H).

5. The rules of Corea must guarantee freedom of religion, freedom of speech and free political activities to all citizens without any foreign interference. There should not be any political persecution or human rights abuse by any governmental organization (see Subchapters 3-B and 3-E).

6. The rules of Corea must be strictly equitable to all regions of the peninsula and suppress any regional or local sectarian violence for the safety of all citizens, in a lawful manner (see Subchapters 3-B, 3-E and 3-G).

7. The Corea government will be obliged to provide every citizen with food, shelter and clothes at a minimum standard without discrimination in regard to any conceivable aspect of each individual.

There may be other fundamental elements that can be added later, when required.

4-B. Governmental Type of the Corea State

The current DPRK in North Korea is basically dictatorial, within Kim's dynastic state operated by Kim Jong Il, the current head of the Korean Workers Party (see Subchapter 3-F), who took the state over from his father Kim Il Sung in 1994. In contrast, South Korea is a Republic state, called Republic of Korea (ROK), maintained on the basis of popular consent, representation and control under the rule of law. Its current president, Roh Moo Hyun, was elected in 2002. The year 2007 is subsequently another presidential election year in the ROK. This proposal will express the basic framework of the new Corea governmental type, and appropriate

governmental officials will determine much details of the new government at a later point within the proposed framework. The new governmental type proposed here is the sole approach, which accommodates the seven basic governing elements, discussed in the previous Subchapter 4-A, in consideration of the current governmental types of the two Korean states as described above.

The **Democratic Constitutional Monarchy** (DCM) is here proposed to be the governmental form of the new Corea state. This modern monarchy is quite different from the old absolute monarchy like the Goryeo dynasty and the Yi Chosun dynasty in Korean history. There are 38 current monarchies in the world, and Corea will be the 39th to this list. The governing body of Corea is to be Parliament, whose members are to be elected directly by the people. The governmental head is the Prime Minister (PM), who will be elected directly or indirectly, and appoint the cabinet members. The King of the new Corea reigns with limited power along with the Parliament, meaning that the King reigns as a symbolic role but does not rule the state. Only the Corean people and the Corean Parliament will rule the Democratic Constitutional Monarchy.

Figure 4 reveals 3 stages leading to the final unified state of Corea. In the first stage, there are two separate states in existence in the year of 2007, as described with major ingredients of each state. In the second stage of retrospect, both states agree to form the unified Democratic Constitutional Monarchy in principle, as proposed here. The unification process is to be executed in the third stage, resulting in a realized Monarchy—Corean State with its fundamental ingredients, as shown in the figure.

As discussed in Subchapters 3-A, 3-B and 3-F, the Corean state has existed virtually over the entire Korean peninsula as indicated in Figure 4, but has not been visible since it was liberated from the Japanese control in 1945. The DPRK and the ROK only then commenced as two separate states over the entire peninsula, which remain in existence. During this period, Kim Il Sung of the Kim dynasty was the eternal president, and Kim Jong Il became the Dear Leader in a form of the personality cult in the North. The current unification plan will combine the two separate states into one monarchy, in continuation of the previous Yi Chosun dynasty with an interruption of 36 years. As a result, General Kim Il Sung will posthumously become the founding King of the Corea Monarchy, called Kim Taejo like Wang Taejo of Goryeo in 936, and Yi Taejo of Yi Chosun dynasty in 1392 (see Subchapter 3-F and Appendices 1 and 2). Similarly, Dr. Rhee Syng Man will be posthumously respected as the first Prime Minister of the Corean state. Then, Kim Jong Il, the current head of the DPRK, will take the second monarch of the Corean monarchy. He will play an initial, strong role during the transition period for the orderly unification

process, to be specified by the new governing Parliament. Similarly, the current president of the ROK, or the next elected president, will take the position of Prime Minister of the new Corean state. The new Prime Minister will construct the new cabinet members and call for a new election in the North. As a result, this proposal presents a win-win unification plan for all Koreans living over the peninsula. For those who find this governmental type difficult to accept, please read again Subchapters 3-A to 3-H in relation to the two goals spelled out in Chapter 1. Other benefits of the proposed plan will be further explained.

During the transition period, the future King Jong Il will have numerous important tasks of dealing effectively with all North Koreans for the successful and rapid reunification. This includes consulting with officials of the new Corea state, to redirect a large number of the current North Korean soldiers from their military mission to fixing North Korea's crumbling infrastructures, much as workers in the Civilian Conservation Corps operated in the US during the Great Depression. They could create incentives for their own domestic industries to open new factories and other facilities in the North which would create jobs and spur economic development. The business men of the South Korea may have experienced through such a difficult economic period and will assist the North Korean counterparts in a logistically efficient manner.

4-C. Prerequisites to the Orderly Unification Process

For this new unification proposal to succeed, the ROK must reach out immediately to the DPRK, whose survival is even arguable at this time, as well as to all other nations whose interest is involved in the stability of East Asia. The ROK must initiate and negotiate all necessary actions in the driver's seat, at an alarming speed before the DPRK collapses in order to achieve the two goals of Chapter 1. Once the DPRK collapses, the unification cost would increase substantially as discussed in the next subchapter. A number of key issues must be worked out prior to the unification process.

1. All South Koreans must overcome any ill feeling toward the North Koreans regarding the Korean War 50+ years ago, and develop brotherly, warm feeling toward them (see Subchapters 3-B and 3-G). The War was a product of the Cold War between two then super powers, one of which has already diminished in the last century.

2. The Congress of the ROK must swiftly push through all necessary legislative bills reflecting the essential elements in Subchapter 4-A and the new governmental type presented in Subchapter 4-B. Most of the work along these lines must have been carried out by

the appropriate agencies of the ROK in its planning programs for years. The ROK should abolish immediately all anti-communist internal security laws, whereas the DPRK must abort the idea of Korean unification on its own terms. Since the Communism of old style has gone to an antique shop, the anti-communist rhetoric must stop among the South Koreans.

3. All of the ROK's agreements, memberships and treaties with foreign nations and world organizations must be arranged to be continued under the new Corea Monarchy, including the mutual defense treaty with the US in effect, if desired. This part will be essential for the South to continue its vibrant economy and to have the North to join the South in the world market under the name of the new Corea state.

4. The ROK government must request the US government to gradually withdraw its forces out of the Korean peninsula within a time table of 3-4 years prior to the completion of the unification process. This is primarily because the security of the new Corea monarchy will be guaranteed by the agreements explained in Chapter 5. With the threat from the DPRK removed consequent to unification, the presence of US forces on the peninsula would no longer serve any material purpose. Also, the ROK's security value to the US would be substantially diminished.

Once the transition team is formed, there may be additional necessary prerequisites.

4-D. Funds Required for Unification and Savings by DCM Unification Process Over Other Processes

Wolf and Akramov (1) made an extensive cost analysis of the three unification scenarios discussed in Chapter 2. They critically showed that there are profound and pervasive uncertainties in each aspect of cost estimation associated with the Korean unification. However, the ROK government must have some plans already in existence to handle humanitarian efforts, economic stabilization, regime absorption, political re-education, job training, administrative and bureaucratic overhaul, military build-down process, social integration, and many other aspects regarding the unification process. The costs for these broad, multi-dimensional issues are difficult to be estimated and have a higher degree of uncertainty. Later in this report, these costs are suggested to be a manageable amount in their total. Regardless, Wolf and Akramov (1) attempted a model simulation for capital costs only on the basis of doubling the North Korean GDP in a relatively short period (four to five pears).

Their models had 9 different parameters, and they ran several hundred cases, resulting in the most significant presentations in Table 5.2, Figures 5.1, 5.2, 5.3 and 5.4 of their book. In their simulation, three important variables governing the capital costs for the unification seem to be the controlling factors, as explained in a crude manner here.

The first one is the preunification ratio between North and South GDP, called GDPPR here. Table 1 (taken from the factbook of CIA, USA, updated on March 15, 2007) shows the PPP(Purchase Power Parity) GDPs of the North and South Korea to be $40 Billion and $1.18 Trillion, respectively. These data have some significant uncertainty. For argument's sake, let us look at them, which amount to a GDPPR of 3.39%. The next parameter is called the Incremental Capital-Output Ratio ICOR, which is the ratio of new investment to additional output. An economy's ICOR includes the cost of both infrastructure and industrial capital. For this unification scenario, the consensus could be that ICOR would most likely be lower than 3, mainly because the unification process would be orderly and a win-win process. A higher ICOR, implying larger capital costs of unification, is likely to be associated with a more conflicted unification. Thirdly, the unification of this type affects the parameter relating to Institutional Reform Strategy (IRS), which embraces economic liberation, property rights, and the rule of law. It could be said that the IRS for this unification scenario may be less than 2. Readers must refer to the book of Wolf and Akramov (1) for more detailed discussions on these parameters.

Table 2 shows the unification capital cost (UCC) in Billion US dollars for the various combinations of IRS (1 to 4) and GDPPR (0.02 to 0.10), for the case of ICOR=3. It is noted that the UCC values increases as GDPPR increases mainly because the absolute doubled values of GDPPR increases rapidly. At GDPPR=0.05, the UCC values are given for ICOR=4 in parenthesis. The UCC values in Table 2 are graphically taken from Figures 5.1 and 5.2 of Wolf and Akramov's book (1) and linearly extrapolated. Thus, there may be some trivial errors in the graphical calculations, which should be insignificant in an absolute sense.

Let's consider three unification scenarios A, B and C of Wolf and Akramov(1) in Chapter 2, which are most recent and representative of all others, in a real setting. The first scenario A was the unification through system evolution and integration, which Park(11) explained to the author as the current unification policy of the ROK during the personal conversation at the meeting with the author in April 2007. Let's consider the North Korean GDP become 10% of South Korean GDP in the next 5 years. Then, the UCC comes as about $360 Billion at IRS=1.5 (see the point A at the Table 2), after 5 years from now. During this 5 years period, 912,500 (500 persons/day x 365 days/year x 5 years) North Koreans would die due to

the human rights abuses under the current regime in the North. The second scenario B was the unification through collapse and absorption. Let's consider that this scenario B would happen after a couple of years from now when the North Korean GDP becomes about 5% of that of the South Korean GDP. Then the UCC of $415 Billion would be at the point B in the Table 2 where IRS is about 2.5 and ICOR is about 4 at its minimum. Let's consider that the third scenario C occurs after a couple of years from now, which is the unification through conflict by some sort of provocation. Then the UCC of more than $605 Billion seems required as shown by the point C in the Table 2.

The UCC values for all of three scenarios would be more than $360 Billion US dollars with the loss of human lives. Now let's consider the proposed case—the orderly and immediate unification scenario by forming the Democratic Constitutional Monarchy (DCM) with a total cooperation from the North Korean leaders and their descendants in exchange with their own securities. Then, the UCC value becomes about $101 Billion at IRS=1.5, ICOR=3 and the current GDPPR of 0.0339 (see DCM point in the Table 2). The most significant conclusion is that the DCM scenario will result in the **savings of more than $250 Billion in the unification capital cost in comparison with those of other unification scenarios**. The current policy makers must understand the significance of this savings on top of the savings of the North Koreans dying daily in hundreds. Moreover, the cost for providing the North Korean leaders and their descendants with their necessary securities would be far less than the savings of more than $250 Billion in the UCC. Let's say that the actual cost for the security providing be $1 Billion for the next 5 years. This amount is so minimal in comparison with the savings of $250 Billion.

The total cost of unification would be dependent on how unification would occur, including the costs of meeting humanitarian demands, stabilization demands, cost for political re-education, job training and system replacement, military build-down process, the demands of social integration, etc. Here Wolf and Akramov (1) focused on the unification capital costs only of doubling the North Korean GDP in a period of four years. It seems to be reasonable to get the total unification cost by adding about the non-capital cost of $120 Billion to that capital cost. Then, for the case of the DCM unification, the total unification cost would be about $220 Billion to be demanded to the government of the new unified Corea over some period.

The conclusion with Table 2 is of utmost importance to all parties involving in the unification process. This unification scenario, with the establishment of the Democratic Constitutional Monarchy, resulted in the total fund requirements, for 3.39% GDPPR, of about $220 Billion.

It would most likely be less than $220 Billion in actuality. These values are significantly lower than previously estimated for other unification scenarios. This significant reduction in the unification cost is directly tied to the merits of this BOLD, EXTRAORDINARY, URGENT, AND WIN-WIN approach proposed here to all Koreans and other nations concerning the Korean Peninsula. The unification cost of $220 Billion is less than 5% of the ROK's cumulative GDP for 4 years. This number is quite favorable and very attractive.

Various ways of sharing the burden of the unification cost can be devised. First of all, the misery of all Koreans for the last century, and the subsequent division of the Korean peninsula, should be attributed to the decisions and actions of the four powerful countries: Japan, China, the US, and Russia (Ryu, 9). Secondly, these countries will have their own national interests in the political stability of the region, as well as in assuring a successful unification process on the peninsula. As a result, a major portion of $220 Billion of the total unification cost should be shared in the form of private or public capital flows by these four countries. It is suggested here that $140 Billion be shared as $60 Billion from the US, $40 Billion from Japan, $20 Billion from China and $20 Billion from Russia. The ROK should share the remaining $80 Billion in negotiation with international financial institutions such as IMF and the World Bank. The ROK government may have other alternatives in preparation of the unification process.

The wide range of Korean unification costs has been reported over the last decade, particularly including analysts at various Korean institutes (Wolf and Akramov, 1). However, the current DCM scenario was not discussed, in which the unification process would be orderly and immediate. This immediate unification process with an order could be the reason why the capital cost for the current DCM scenario is far lower than the cost of any other.

4-E. Benefits from the Immediate Korea Unification

There are numerous benefits from the peaceful and immediate unification through the formation of the Democratic Constitutional Monarchy. Also, the current political and economic climate among the powerful nations has been cordial such that the stability of the region should easily be achieved through the effort of the United Nations. Here are the major benefits:

1. The lives of the North Koreans dying in hundreds everyday will be saved. This is the most urgent humanitarian mission which must be addressed immediately by both South Koreans and North Koreans,

further supported by the participating countries in the United Nations.

2. The proposed governmental form being the Democratic Constitutional Monarchy will provide security to the North Korean leaders and their descendants, who will, in exchange, cooperatively assist the new Corea state for the orderly unification of the two Korean states (See Subchapter 4-B). Unlike the chaotic situation in Iraq, the problems of the Corea state will be manageable in the spirit of cooperation among most citizens of the new state.

3. As shown in the previous subchapter, the savings of the unification capital cost will exceed $100 Billion, possibly more than $200 Billion, with the proposed mode of the orderly and immediate unification. This savings are huge in comparison with the actual cost for providing the securities to the North Korean leaders and their descendants.

4. There will no longer be national or international animosity over the Korean peninsula by two non-aggression agreements, which will provide every concerned nation with the stability of the East Asia. (See Chapter 5). Furthermore, all of the WMD possibly existing in the peninsula will come under the supervision of the United Nations.

5. As implied by the current ties of the South Korea with China, Japan, Russia and the US, the new state of Corea Monarchy will basically neutral and peaceful.

6. The wealth of the new Corea state will be immensely increased, which will be delightfully enjoyed freely and equally by all citizens on the peninsula. Table 3 shows this increase.

Initially, there will be at least two concerned drawbacks. First, a minority portion of the South Koreans is so anti-Communist oriented that they would be hard to accept the notion of the new governmental type with Kim Jong Il as their symbolic King. The same minority group would resist accepting the Communist political party as a legitimate political party as any other party. However, as mentioned earlier, the Communism of old style had gone to a antique shop. Most importantly, the majority of the population of the unified state is certainly guaranteed to seek democracy, freedom, and liberty as current South Koreans do.

Peace Be With the World !
A Plea for Human Society To Come Together/Unite !

Chapter 5

STABILITY OF EAST ASIA
THROUGH THE UNITED NATIONS

In the 21st century, one of the United Nations' remaining goals is to have its member nations maintain world peace and avoid any military conflict, intentional or unintentional, in its cause. It is here proposed to achieve the stability of East Asia by two agreements among the member nations of the United Nations. The two proposals are to be discussed within the context of the recent history over the Korean peninsula and their presentation follows.

As discussed in Subchapter 3-B, the Korean War was a direct conflict of the Cold War between the US-led western block and the pro-Soviet bloc. Now, more than 60 i years after the Korean War armistice, a UN command is still present on the Korean peninsula, which is the main force behind the conflict perpetuating the inhumane, dictatorial Kim dynasty in the North. The Cold War ended more than a decade ago, and the US remains to be only the super power. As a result, to immediately save the lives of North Koreans dying daily in hundreds, this Korean conflict must first end (see Subchapter 3-E). The human rights issue in the DPRK should be the primary goal, which deserves immediate attention according to the Charter of the UN, and to the mission statement of the ROK at the UN.

The ROK mission statement has said to remain "firm in its two goals of establishing permanent peace on the peninsula and contributing to the

stability and prosperity of the region and beyond". It also is well known that permanent peace is not possible on the peninsula as long as the DMZ zone, dividing the one nation and one Korean race into two parts, exists, and the US forces remain on the peninsula, like the current situation. The last section laid out how to achieve the first of its two goals—the permanent peace on the peninsula, which means the peaceful unification of two Korean states. Of course, there will be an initial chaotic period after the unification process begins. However, there will be a calm sea of peace after the big wave of minimal turbulence. Time is of the essence because North Koreans may be dying in hundreds due to unacceptable human rights abuses. These lives have been sacrificed for the prosperity of the ROK economy, but they should not be sacrificed any longer.

The second firm goal of the ROK mission statement is said to be the stability and the prosperity of the region and beyond. The stability of East Asia can be achieved by the following two proposals to be signed under the auspice of the United Nations, and therefore regional prosperity should easily follow.

5-A. The Guarantee by the United Nations to the Unified Corea

This first proposal will provide the unified Corea with non-aggression security by China, Japan, Russia and the United States under the auspice of the United Nations, which is coupled with the stability of the East Asian Region. Let us look at the historical reason, which would explain the necessity of a security agreement.

From the onset of the Yi Chosun dynasty in 1392 to the modern era, the Korean people have both suffered and benefited, voluntarily and involuntarily, from the interactions with its four neighboring countries: China, Japan, Russia (the former USSR) and United States(the US). Ryu (9) and Appendix 1 revealed very clearly the factual presentations of each of these countries' involvement with Korea as they relate to wars and domination over the Korean peninsula. Among these four nations, there were three treaties or agreements made during the last 150 years regarding the Korean peninsula. These resulted in the immense misery inflicted on the Korean people. The three previous agreements will be briefly revealed here to show the necessity of the new agreements to be proposed for the region's stability after the Korean unification begins.

1). The Tientsin Treaty between China and Japan in1885
On April 18, 1885, Japan and China entered into an agreement to decide who would dominate and control Korea, as historically was

the case, with Korean opinion ignored. In this Tientsin Treaty, both Chinese and Japanese governments agreed to withdraw military forces from Korea within four months. They were to also give advanced notification should the other party find it necessary to send its troops back to the Korean peninsula. Though both countries did withdraw, China continued, as she had done throughout history, to intervene in Korean domestic affairs.

Once the treaty was in effect, Korean citizens rebelled against corruption throughout the final years of the Yi Chosun dynasty, which included the culminating Donghak rebellion in 1894. These rebellions brought Chinese military intervention, because, as in the past, the Korean government asked China for assistance. However, contrary to the Tientsin Treaty, China did not inform Japan that she was sending troops into Korea. When Japan discovered this, she sent troops to Korea and declared war on July 25, 1894, against the Chinese forces in the Gulf of Asan, a western Korean port. This Sino-Japanese War ended with Japanese victory in February of the following year, which was followed in 1905 by Japan's victory over the Russians in the Russo-Japanese war and the Japanese annexation of Korea, all leading to WWII.

2). Taft-Katsura Memorandum between the US and Japan in 1905

Regarding the Korean peninsula, the US made an important move with the Taft-Katsura Memorandum, which later became significant in terms of Korean welfare. This memorandum (also called an agreement) was signed on July 29, 1905 by the US Secretary of War, William Howard Taft, who later became an US President, and the Prime Minister of Japan, Katsura Taro. In this agreement, the US recognized Japan's sphere of influence in Korea; in exchange, Japan recognized the US sphere of influence in the Philippines. This secret agreement was not publicized until 1924. It is believed that the Taft-Katsura Agreement violated the earlier Korean-American Treaty of Amity and Commerce signed at Incheon on May 22, 1882, and that it completely disregarded Korean security and sovereignty issues. This agreement can be viewed as the direct cause of Korean colonization by Japan, which inflicted unforgettable misery on the Korean people. Furthermore, Japan eventually expanded its imperialism throughout the whole region, and carried out the WWII.

3). The Moscow Agreement between the US and the USSR in 1945

At the post-WWII Moscow Conference of the allied powers in December 1945, an agreement was initially reached that Korea would pass through a seven-year period of trusteeship to prepare her for

mature independence. However, Korean opposition was so strong that the proposal was eventually dropped. Instead, the Joint U.S.-U.S.S.R. Commission was formed to occupy Korea. The Joint Commission tried in vain to create a solution to the problem of unifying Korea, but it soon became clear that this was not possible. The continued occupation of the land by the two opposing military forces had reached a stage where unification was far beyond the powers of the Joint Commission. Subsequently, North Korea and South Korea were formed as two different states, the Korean War broke out, and the DMZ truce was signed, leading to a temporary and fragile peace. Since that time, US armed forces have remained in South Korea.

All of the three agreements over the Korean peninsula were reached and executed only for the benefit of the foreign governments in the pursuit of their own interests in the region. These were done with total disregard for the wishes of the Korean people. These nations have used the Korean peninsula as a battleground, and as an exploitable source in pursuing their own interests in the region. Koreans have never been strong enough to defend their country or to attack any nation, but have been forced to yield to the demands of others. As a result, these foreign nations have historically inflicted unacceptable misery on the Korean people in the name of humane assistance. Now, the Korean people are requesting the governments of these four powerful nations to sign the proposed, non-aggression agreement for the stability of the East Asian region.

Looking at today's security environment among the four major powers, there is no resemblance to that of the Cold War. China and Russia are both conventional great powers, but they do not pose malignantly expansionist threats to international peace or to America's security (Carpenter and Bandow,10). Japan has no incentive to disrupt the current arrangement with other states or superpowers, particularly in their economic relationship. As the worldwide conciliatory atmosphere warms after the Cold War era, and as the four major regional powers come to increasingly desire the stability in this region, it is the optimal time to request signature of the proposed non-aggression pact, Proposal #1 (see below),over the Korean peninsula.

Proposal #1. Non-aggression Guarantee on Korean Peninsula

The nations undersigned below shall not intentionally or unintentionally, attack the Korean peninsula, or provoke any conflict with military forces, regardless of any circumstances, for the next century. This security guarantee must be signed under the auspice of the United Nations by

the governmental representatives of the Peoples' Republic of China, Japan, Russia, and the United States of America. This will be coupled with additional guarantee that all foreign forces are to be withdrawn from the peninsula within an agreed time period, as discussed in Chapter 4.

5-B. The Guarantee by the Unified Corea to the United Nations

In receipt of the security guarantee from the four powerful nations under the auspice of the United Nations, the unified Corea needs, in exchange, to provide the United Nations with a non-aggression, direct or indirect, security to those nations. This second proposal is to be initially developed below with some current facts in a historical perspective.

The Korean history of the last 2,000 years indicates there were many internal fights and revolts among different factions within the Korean peninsula. But this same history also clearly shows that no Korean kingdom or state ever attacked or occupied a neighboring country. One can imply from these historical observations that the unified Corea is unlikely to attack any neighbor in the future unless provoked by an external force. The major culprit of Korean misery over the last thousand years, which resulted from foreign domination, has been the weakness of the Korean military. During the last 50 plus years, since the DMZ truce of the Korean War, South Korea has developed economic strength in the world market under the protection of the joint defense agreement with the US, while North Korea has developed military strength through, it is assumed, producing nuclear arms. Once both of these newly developed strengths are combined into the unified Corea, the newly acquired military strength must be kept under the UN's supervision in order to deter any party from encroaching again onto the peninsula. Corea will ultimately benefit from this arrangement.

Numerous current concerns have been raised regarding the Weapons of Mass Destruction (WMD) possibly possessed by the DPRK. The followings are the most recent, known facts:

— 7/4/2006: six missiles test-fired, including a long-range Taepodong-2, the 7th one followed the next day.
— 10/9/2006: a small nuclear bomb tested in the North triggered a seismic event of 4.2 in Richter scale.
— 2/13/2007: the fifth round of the six-party talks concluded with an agreement shutting down the Yongbyon reactor in exchange for fuel aid.

The DPRK is widely believed to possess a substantial arsenal of chemical and biological weapons and also the delivery systems of the WMD in a limited range. According to North Korea, this arsenal may be required as future deterrent from foreign invasion. This deterrent aspect was clearly stated by Pakistani on 3/22/07 when Pakistani military test fired nuclear capable cruise missiles. Considering the historical events for the last 150 years, Corea needs such deterrent more so than ever.

The following is proposal #2, to be signed by the representative of the unified Corea, for the stability of the East Asian region under the auspice of the United Nations.

Proposal #2. Non-aggression Guarantee by Unified Corea

The unified Corea shall not intentionally or unintentionally, attack any other surrounding nations or provoke any conflict with military forces, regardless of any circumstances on the peninsula, for the next century. Also, the agreement shall include all WMD arsenals existing in the Korean peninsula put under the UN's supervision. This security guarantee must be signed under the auspice of the United Nations by the unified Corea governmental representative.

These two proposals #1 and #2 should be prepared in a legal format for the guaranteed stability of the East Asian region. Along with the plans for the Korean unification, and the formation of the unified Corea, the two international agreements shall be executed by the representatives' signatures of the five following nations; Peoples' Republic of China, Japan, Russia, the United States of America, and Corea. Corea shall be represented by the Prime Minister of Corea, in consultation with Corea's King of the Democratic Constitutional Monarchy.

As stated in Chapter 1, this proposed plan has two goals to achieve: the immediate rescue of the North Koreans dying daily by the hundreds, and the stability of the East Asian region. The first goal will be attained by the immediate unification of the Korean peninsula, which is sufficed by the formation of the Democratic Constitutional Monarchy, Corea state, over the Korean peninsula. This is depicted in Figure 4. The people of the Monarchy will be symbolically represented by the King and the country will be governed by the parliament and the Prime Minister with its cabinet members.

The second goal, which is stability of the East Asian region, will be attained by two proposed agreements under the auspice of the United Nations, as summarized in Figure 5. The two proposals must be agreed to and signed by the four powerful nations: Peoples' Republic of China,

Japan, Russia and the United States of America as well as Corea. To achieve these goals, the majority of Koreans must agree on this forward movement. This is reasonably attainable, in that the two goals above are well within the realm of the UN's charter: world peace and human rights. In conclusion of this proposal are the reconciliation messages below with an important aspect that TIME IS OF THE ESSENCE TO SAVE HUMAN LIVES BEING LOST EACH DAY.

Peace Be With the World !
A Plea for Human Society To Come Together/Unite !

Chapter 6

RECONCILATION MESSAGES IN CONCLUSION

6-A. Message to the People of South Korea

The utmost important and urgent mission of all Koreans is to rescue the North Koreans dying daily by the hundreds. As may be well understood, the DPRK is a state that appears to be functioning on a sort of "life-support" basis by tactically negotiating provisional extensions for its lease on life. Given the nature of the North Korean state, those negotiations are highly circumscribed. For the current dismal economy of the DPRK, an extensive commercial interaction with South Korea and other nations may help resuscitate the North Korean economy. But apparently the DPRK leaders, fearing that such contacts may destabilize their system, have denied that option. Meanwhile not only more North Koreans are dying daily, but a large portion of the North Koreans live every day amid violence, at home from an abhorrent family dictatorship and abroad from the half-century long threat from the mightiest nation on this planet—America. It is time that the ROK makes a **bold and extraordinary initiative** toward the orderly Korean unification, as proposed here in Chapters 3, 4 and 5.

There are several merits of the immediate and orderly unification. The current North Korea is here said to be far less dangerous than the collapsed North Korea absorbed by the South Korea without order in the country (see Subchapters 3-G and 3-H). This order will come only from the cooperative assistance by the North Korean leaders in executing the unification process

designed for the rapid growth of the North Korean economy. In return, the security of the North Korean leaders and their descendants is to be guaranteed by the formation of the Democratic Constitutional Monarchy, as explained in Chapter 4. This rapid and peaceful unification process should be the win-win, cost-saving proposal, which will also immediately save the North Korean lives dying daily by the hundreds. All South Koreans must embrace the northern sisters and brothers who are in grave trouble, and must leave behind all antagonizing, anti-communist feelings. All political parties in the South Korea must unit together behind this historical and bold project by suppressing personal greed and political ambitions for the future betterment of all Coreans.

6-B. Message to the People of North Korea

As is the message to the people of South Korea, the utmost important and urgent mission of all Koreans is to rescue the North Koreans dying daily in hundreds. The DPRK leaders must recognize these unnecessary deaths, primarily a result of the unworkable political system of the DPRK, Kim dynasty and its dismal economy as shown in Table 1 and Figure 1. The life of the state will be finite, in reflection of the current world trend, in which Communism becomes an antique of the waning-down ideology. Though capitalism possesses numerous social drawbacks, it provides all citizens of a democratic country with freedom and liberty in the very least. This is currently enjoyed by the citizens of the ROK, which is the 13TH economic power in the world. In contrast, a large percentage of North Koreans live without such freedom and liberty every day amidst violence.

The North Korean leaders must give up their intent to unify the Korean peninsula on their own terms and submit their political power to the genuine formation of the unified Corea, as discussed in Chapter 4. In doing so, North Korean citizens will be freed to aid in the rapid growth of its economy, by bringing South Korea's free market economic system into the North. In the meantime, the North Korean leaders will enjoy their future security within the framework of the proposed Democratic Constitutional Monarchy of Corea (see Chapter 4). All citizens in the North will live equally to the citizens in the South under the protection of the rules of law in the new Corea Monarchy.

6-C. Message to the Neighboring Countries: China, Japan, Russia, and the United States

Both religious and nonreligious people question how "God" created a world full of innocent suffering, and then possibly demand their loyalty,

unjustly dying, for the sake of this "God". Imperialistic and expanding nations have constantly been battled in the name of security and freedom, and have been finding enemies, now down to North Korea even in hunger. Several decades ago, Albert Einstein said with lamentation "Great powers do not act on the basis of facts only, but manufacture the facts to serve their purposes and force their will on smaller nations" (Lee, 8). They have victimized people living in small countries most unacceptably and inhumanely, Korea being a prime example. It is the time these great powers stop any further aggression.

Regarding the Korean peninsula during the last 150 years, three specific agreements were made among the four powerful countries: China, Japan, Russia, and the United States. They are the Tientsin Treaty between China and Japan in 1885, Taft-Katsura Memorandum between the US and Japan in 1905, and The Moscow Agreement between the US and the USSR in 1945 (see Subchapter 5-B). These agreements determined the fate of the Korean people, completely disregarding their wishes, and creating such misery among Koreans. These treaties typically resulted in follow-up wars, and the resultant Korean misery became collateral civilian deaths in hundreds of thousands, mass property destruction, and total inhumane actions of foreign occupiers. Over 50 years later, the Korean War has still not been resolved and the unbearable hostility of the two parties continues at the DMZ zone between the North Korean soldiers and the US-led UN forces. There are currently 28,000 US solders still in South Korea. It has been questioned as to how much more time will pass until the end of this misery is visible, meanwhile many Koreans continue to die. The time is now for these nations to let the Korean peninsula have eternal peace. It is also recognized here that these countries are obliged to contribute substantially to the financial burden in achieving the rapid and orderly unification process proposed in Chapter 4.

The plan proposed here (see Chapter 5) contains two two-way guarantees under the auspice of the United Nations for the stability of the East Asian region:

#1. Security Guarantee on Korean peninsula by four nations-Peoples' Republic of China, Japan, Russia, and the US (Subchapter 5-A);
#2. Non-aggression Guarantee by the unified Corea (Subchapter 5-B) to other nations.

These two agreements are urged to be signed concurrently with the beginning of the Korea unification process for the sake of the world peace, more specifically to save the lives being lost daily in hundreds.

6-D. Message to the Secretary General Ban Ki-moon and the General Assembly President Sheikha Haya Rashed Al Khalifa of the United Nations

Here is copied the Preamble of the United Nations.

WE THE PEOPLES OF THE UNITED NATIONS DETERMINED

> ➤ to save succeeding generations from the scourge of war, which twice in our lifetime has brought untold sorrow to mankind, and
> ➤ to reaffirm faith in fundamental human rights, in the dignity and worth of the human person, in the equal rights of men and women and of nations large and small, and
> ➤ to establish conditions under which justice and respect for the obligations arising from treaties and other sources of international laws can be maintained, and
> ➤ to promote social progress and better standards of life in larger freedom.

Madam President and Mr. Secretary-General must apply these UN determinations to the case of Korean Conflict, which has been lasting more than 6 decades long. The current human rights abuses in North Korea (see Subchapter 3-E) results in the daily deaths of North Koreans in hundreds, not just a few. Several hundreds of children, women and men die in North Korea today, and will die tomorrow, and the next day.

To save these lives immediately, the comprehensive plan outlined in this booklet submits to you two concrete propositions:

1. *Orderly Korea Unification*, that is bold, urgent, extraordinary, and win-win to all peoples concerned (see Chapter 4), and
2. *Guarantee of Stability in East Asia* through the United Nations (see Chapter 5), which will derive from two proposals;

    Proposal #1. Non-aggression guarantee on Korean Peninsula for the next century by Peoples' Republic of China, Japan, Russia, and the United States of America (see Subchapter 5-A). Also guaranteed is the withdrawal of all foreign forces from the peninsula within an agreed time period.

    Proposal #2. Non-aggression Guarantee by the unified Corea to other Nations for the next century (see Subchapter 5-B). Also all of the WMD, which may be existing in the peninsula, is to be put under the UN's supervision.

When these two propositions become a reality, we the people will see

> - all citizens of the Korean peninsula be free and enjoy the freedom and liberty currently enjoyed by the citizens of South Korea,
> - the Korean peninsula unified into a state of Democratic Constitutional Monarchy—Corea,
> - the stability and prosperity of the East Asian region firm and marching forward,
> - no nations in this world concerning human rights abuses in the peninsula and possible threat of WMD possibly existing in the peninsula, and finally
> - people of all nations be welcome in the new state of Corea and be able to ride a happy train from Busan, tip of Corea, through Mt. Baekdu, to Siberia or China.

Madam President and Mr. Secretary-General! Please help the world to save these dying citizens of the world and make your resolutions in combining your immediate efforts and so forming an exploration committee in order to accomplish the two goals set out in the beginning of the propositions—ORDERLY KOREA UNIFICATION AND THE GUARANTEE OF STABILITY IN EAST ASIA.

As shown in the "Letter to the Members of the UN Exploratory Committee (UNEC)" following the Preface in the beginning of this report, the UNEC is suggested to consist of 11 members of the United Nations for embarking on this giant step towards the Korean unification. The 11 members are listed as below:

Representative of the United Nations, Chairperson,
Representative of Norway, Vice Chairperson,
Representative of India, Vice Chairperson,
Representative of German, Unification Process Advisor,
Representative of Singapore, Unification Process Advisor,
Representative of South Korea, Project Manager,
Representative of North Korea, Deputy Manager,
Representative of China, Unification Fund Advisor,
Representative of Japan, Unification Fund Advisor,
Representative of Russia, Project Advisor, and
Representative of the United States, Project Advisor.

It is here suggested that the UN immediately initiates the formation of the UNEC for conducting a feasibility study on the proposal outlined in this report.

The mission of the UNEC is threefold.

1. Each one of the 11 UNEC members is to understand the proposal outlined in this report, clearly and unquestionably. For this step, the author of the proposal is available to present the details of the proposed items in person or via phone or email to the UNEC members, individually or collectively.
2. The members of the UNEC are to carry out their feasibility studies on the proposed items, in consultation with appropriate governmental agencies of the nations involved.
3. Upon the completion of their feasibility studies, the Chairperson will call a final meeting where the UNEC's recommendation is to be made. If the recommendation is positive, the UNEC is to produce a road map toward the successful completion of the proposed items. If the recommendation becomes negative or needs some modifications on the proposal, the UNEC's final report is written in that effect.

Time is of essence here to save the lives dying daily in North Korea, due to the human rights abuses by the regime of the North Korea. The UNEC member should meet the first official meeting on the earliest, designated date.

Peace Be With the World !
A Plea for Human Society To Come Together/Unite !

References

1. Wolf, Charles Jr and Kamil Akramov, 2005 "North Korean Paradoxes: Circumstances, Costs, and Consequences of Korean Unification; pp.71, Rand Corporation, Santa Monica, CA, USA

2. Bennett, Bruce, 2006, N Korea Policy Options; Commentary (appeared in United Press International on 11/28/2006), Rand Corporation, Santa Monica, CA, USA

3. Head, Tom, 2007, Human Rights in North Korea—North Korean Human Rights Abuses, www.civilliberty.about.com/od/internationalhumanrights/p/northkorea101.htm.

4. Refugees International, 2007, www.refugeesinternational.org/section/publications/nk-scope/

5. Martin, Bradley K, 2004, Under the Loving Care of the Fatherly Leader-North Korea and the Kim Dynasty, pp.868, St. Martin's Press, New York, USA

6. Wolf, Charles Jr., 2006, Tokyo's Leverage Over Pyongyang; Commentary on 11/21/2006, www.rand.org/commentary/112106AWSJ.html

7. Eberstadt, Nicholas, 2007, The End of North Korea, American Enterprise Institute Press, http://partners.nytimes.com/books/first/e/eberstadt-korea.html

8. Lee, Hwal-woong, Did the U.S. want a Korean War? Feb 2-3, 2007, Korean Unification Conference, Claremont Graduate University, CA, www.coreapeace.com/news/news.php?code=30527.

9. Ryu, J., Is North Korea A Threat to Americans?; March 3, 2007, pp.13, NWPF-RPT20070303, www.newworldpeacefoundation.org.

10. Carpenter, Ted G and Bandow, Doug,The Korean Conundrum; 2004, pp.218, Palgrave, New York, N. Y.
11. Park Sang-Jin, Consul at Korean Consulate General in Los Angeles, Personal conversation on April 3, 2007.

List of Figures

Figure 1. Current economic situation of six nations concerning the Korean peninsula, taken from Table 1, updated on March 15, 2007.

Figure 2. The chronological view of the history on the peninsula until the formation of the two separate states on the peninsula.

Figure 3. DPRK and ROK were born by adoption process when the Cold War began between two superpowers; USSR and USA.

Figure 4. This figure shows the current situation of the DPRK and the ROK, the proposed unified government in retrospect, and the results of the unification process.

Figure 5. The summary of Chapter 5 providing the United Nations with two-way guarantee of stability in East Asia.

RUSSIA	United States
President	President
Vladimir Putin	**George W. Bush**
GDP per Capita	GDP per Capita
$12,100	$43,500

China	Japan
President	Prime Minister
Hu Jintao	**Shinzo Abe**
GDP per Capita	GDP per Capita
$7,600	$33,100

South Korea, ROK

President
Roh Moo-hyun
GDP per Capita
$24,200

North Korea, DPRK

Chairman
Kim Jong Il
GDP per Capita
$1,800

Figure 1. Current economic situation of six nations concerning the Korean peninsula, taken from Table 1, updated on March 15, 2007.

조선—*History of Han Guk aka COREA*

Dan Gun Period—Dating back to 2333 year B.C.

Three Kingdoms Period—Start of 1st Century
> *Goguryeo* in the Southern Manchuria and the Northern peninsula,
> *Baekje* in the Southwestern part of the peninsula, &
> *Silla* in the Southeastern part of the peninsula.

Unified Silla—Middle of 6th Century

(current boundary of the peninsula)

Goryeo Dynasty   founded by General Wang Geon,
(936-1392)   King Taejo of Goryeo

Yi Chosun Dynasty   founded by General Yi Seong Gye,
(1392-1910)   King Taejo of Yi Chosun

(Sino-Japanese War & Russo-Japanese War)

Japanese Colony—	1910 to 1945—	End of WW II

USSR	(See Figure 3)	USA
	Controlled and divided the peninsula	
	By *adoption* process by force 1945-1948	

DPRK-Kim Dynasty   The Republic of Korea- **ROK**
(North Korea) founded by   (South Korea) formed by
General Kim Il Sung—   Dr. Rhee Sygn Man—
1st Dictator in 1948   1st Elected President in 1948

Figure 2. The chronological view of the history on the peninsula until the
formation of the two separate states on the peninsula.

| World War II Ended and Cold War Began in 1945 |

| USSR | vs | USA |
Joseph Stalin   Harry S. Truman

Pro-Communist Bloc   Pro-Western Bloc

| *ADOPTION PROCESS, NOT MARRIAGE* |
| Produced Puppet Governments by force in 1948. |

| DPRK | vs | ROK |
Democratic People's   Republic of Korea
Republic of Korea
(North Korea)   (South Korea)

Kim Il Sung   Rhee Syng Man
Communist Dictator   Elected President

Figure 3. DPRK and ROK were born by adoption process when the Cold
    War began between two superpowers; USSR and USA.

GOVERNMENTAL TYPE OF UNIFIED COREA :
DEMOCRATIC CONSTITUTIONAL MONARCHY

Stage #1   2007 Situation over the peninsula

North Korea DPRK	South Korea ROK
Million+ military force	World 13th economic power
Nuclear arsenal	600,000+ armed forces
GDP per capita $1,800	GDP per capita $24,200
Human rights abuses	US forces in the land
Dictator—Kim Jong Il	President Roh Moo-hyun
(Absolute King of Kim dynasty)	(elected by people)

Stage #2   In Retrospect

Democratic Constitutional Monarchy as Proposed for Corea (existed since 1948 but not visible)

Symbolic King	*Parliament Governs Corea*
Ceremonial only	People Elects Its Members
Founding Monarch—	and Prime Minister (PM).
Kim Il Sung	Founding PM—Rhee Syng Man

Stage #3   In Execution of

Orderly and Peaceful Unification as Proposed

Unified Corea: Democratic Constitutional Monarchy

2nd Monarch—	Prime Minister-
Kim Jong Il	Roh Moo Hyun or newly elected President

Basic Elements of Corea
1. ROK system over the entire peninsula,
2. No human rights abuses in peninsula,
3. Beginning of guaranteed stability in East Asia,
4. Freedom and liberty to all citizens of Corea

Figure 4. This figure shows the current situation of the DPRK and the ROK, the proposed unified government in retrospect, and the results of the unification process.

Two-Way Agreements for the stability in East Asia

AGREEMENT #1. Non-aggression Guarantee on Korean Peninsula
for the next century, to be signed by the
Governments of China, Japan, Russia, and USA
Under the Auspice of the United Nations,

with additional guarantee that
all of foreign forces stationing in the
peninsula will be withdrawn from the
peninsula within an agreed time period.

AGREEMENT #2. Non-aggression Guarantee to Other Nations
for the next century, to be signed by the
Government of the Unified Corea

with additional Guarantee that
All of WMD existing in the peninsula will be
put under the United Nations' Supervision.

Figure 5. The summary of Chapter 5 providing the United Nations with the guarantee of stability in East Asia.

List of Tables

Table 1. Comparative Facts of 6 Nations: S. Korea, N. Korea, China, Japan, Russia, and the United States

Table 2. Unification Capital Cost

Table 3. Comparison of Unified Corea with two Current Koreas

Table 1. Comparative Facts of 6 Nations

Country	South Korea	North Korea	China	Japan	Russia	United States
General						
1. Government Type	Republic	One-Man Dictator Communist State	Communist State - Market Economy	Constitutional Monarchy	Federation	Federal Republic
2. Land Area Sq Km	98,190	120,410	9,326,410	374,744	16,995,800	9,161,923
3. Population	48,846,823	23,113,019	1,313,973,713	127,463,611	142,893,540	298,444,215
4. Population Growth Rate	0.42%	0.84%	0.59%	0.94%	-0.37%	0.91%
5. Religion No Affiliation	46%	Traditionally	Majority	Shinto and	50+%	10%
Christian	26%	Buddhist and	3-4%	Buddhist 84%	2%	78%
Buddhist	26%	Confucian	Main Relig.		Orthodox 20-%	
Others	2%		Muslim 1-2%	16%		12%
6. Language	Korean	Korean	Mandarin, etc	Japanese	Russian	English
7. Capital	Seoul	Pyongyang	Beijing	Tokyo	Moscow	Washington D.C.
8. Independence	8/15/1945	8/15/1945	221 bbc	660 B.C.	1991 from Soviets	7/4/1776
9. Next Election	12/07-President	8/08-Legislative	3/2008	Varied	12/2007	11/4/08-President
Economy						
10. GDP						
Purchasing Power Parity	$1.18 Trillion	$40 Billion	$10 Trillion	$4.22 Trillion	$1.723 Trillion	$12.98 Trillion
Official Exchange Rate	$897.4 Billion	Unofficial Estimate	$2.512 Trillion	$4.911 Trillion	$733 Billion	$13.22 Trillion
Real Growth	4.8%	1%	10.5%	2.8%	6.6%	3.4%
Per Capita	$24,200	$1,800	$7,600	$33,100	$12,100	$43,500
11. Composition by Sector %						
Agriculture	3	30	11.9	1.6	5.3	0.9
Industrial	46	34	48.1	25.3	36.6	20.4
Service	52	36	40.0	73.1	58.2	78.6
13. Unemployment Rate %	3.3	NA	4.2	4.1	6.6	4.8
14. Inflation Rate %	2.2	NA	1.5	0.4	10.0	2.5
15. Budget	$201 Billion	NA	$489.6 Billion	$1.639 Trillion	$222.2 Billion	$2.409 Trillion
16. Public Debt-%of GDP	31.9	NA	22.1	176.2	8.0	64.7
17. Oil Consumption (million bbl/day)	2.149	0.025	6.534	5.578	2.5	20.73
18. Current Account Balance	$2 Billion	NA	$179.1 Billion	$174.4 Billion	$105.3 Billion	-$862.3 Billion
19. Export, $Billion	326 fob	1.34 fob	974 fob	590.3 fob	317.6 fob	1,024 fob
Import	309.3 fob	2.6 cif	778 fob	524.1 fob	171.5 fob	1,869 fob
20. Reserves of Foreign Exchange & Gold	$239 Billion	NA	$1.034 Trillion	$864.9 Billion	$69.19 Billion	$314.5 Billion
21. Debt-External	$249.4 Billion	$12 Billion	$305.6 Billion	$1.547 Trillion	$287.4 Billion	$10.04 Trillion

22. Currency	Won-krw	Won-kpw	Yuan	Yen	Russian Ruble	Dollar
23. Exchange Rate to $	955.3	141	7.97	116	27.5	1

Military

24. Military Expenditure (% of GDP)	3.0% of FY05	NA	4.3%	0.9%	NA	4.06% of FY03
25. Fit Manpower Male (2/8/07 data)	10,115,817	4,810,831	281,240,272	22,234,663	21,049,651	54,609,050
Female	9,721,914	4,853,270	269,025,517	21,494,947	29,056,021	54,696,706

Ref: *www.cia.gov/cia/publications/factbook*, Updated 3/15/2007

Table 2. Unification Capital Cost in Billions, for ICOR=3

GDPPR	IRS=1		2		3	4
0.02	31		84		137	190
0.03	54		136		218	300
		DCM				
0.04	77		188		299	410
0.05	100		240		380	520
ICOR=4<	(130)		(320)	B	(510)	C (700)>
0.06	123		292		461	630
0.08	169		396		623	850
0.10	215	A	500		785	

Table 2 shows the unification capital cost (UCC) in Billion US dollars for the various combinations of IRS and GDPPR, for the case of ICOR=3, where ICOR is the incremental capital-output ratio, IRS stands for Institutional Reform strategy, and GDPPR is the preunification ratio of North/South GDP. At GDPPR=0.05, the UCC are given for ICOR=4 in parenthesis. The values for the unification capital costs are graphically taken from Figures 5.1 and 5.2 of Wolf and Akramov's book (1) and linearly extrapolated. The UCC values at points A (360), B (415), C (605) and DCM (101) are corresponding to scenarios A, B, C and DCM (see the text), respectively.

Table 3. Comparison of Corea with Two Current Koreas

	North Korea	South Korea	Corea
Population (06 est)	23,113,019	48,846,823	71,959,842
Capitol	Pyongyang	Seoul	Kaeseong OR Panmunjeom
Language	Hangul	Hangul	Hangul
Area sq km—Land	120,410	98,190	218,600
Land Value only** (in Trillion)	$2.4082	$1.9638	$4.372

** It is assumed that the value of one sq km is $20,000 per sq km. This value may be quite lower than the actual value. It should be also noted that the Corea is located at the most desirable, real estate in the world.

List of Appendices

Appendix 1. History of Korea for the last 2000 years

    A. Description of the Korean Peninsula
    B. Origin of the Korean People
    C. A Brief History of Korea up to the Fourteenth Century
    D. Korean History for the Last 500 Years

Appendix 2. Founders of Korea Kingdoms or States

    A. General Wang Geon (877-943)—Taejo of Goryeo (936-943)
    B. General Yi Seong Gye (Lee Sung-Gye;1335-1408)—Taejo of Chosun(1392-1398) also known as Yi Dynasty
    C. General Kim Il Sung (1912-1994)—President of North Korea (DPRK)(1972-1994)
    D. Dr. Rhee Syng Man (1875-1965)—President of South Korea (ROK)(1948-1960)

Appendix 1

HISTORY OF KOREA FOR THE LAST 2000 YEARS

First, Korean peninsula and people are described in a brief way. Next, the Korea history for the last 2000 years is described in a cursory manner here, with the emphasis on the history for the last 500 years.

A. Description of the Korean Peninsula

Korea, also known as Taehan Minguk, was frequently called Hanguk, and the inhabitants preferred to call it Chosun, "The Land of the Morning Calm". The Korean peninsula, with 3,300 islands, has an area of 220,845 square kilometers. It is bounded by the Yalu River, the Duman River and the Baekdu Mt. on its north and surrounded on three sides by the Yellow Sea toward China, the South Sea and the East Sea (aka the Sea of Japan) toward Japan.

At the end of the World War II, the peninsula was divided into **two Koreas** by an agreement between the US and the USSR in total disregard of the Korean people's wishes; North Korea was named as the Democratic People's Republic of Korea (DPRK), with her capital at Pyongyang, and South Korea became the Republic of Korea (ROK), with her capital in Seoul. In 1953 when the Korean War ended, the communist forces of North Korea and the US-backed UN forces representing South Korea signed a truce establishing a Demarcation Military Zone (DMZ) along an agreed line that divides the two countries. This DMZ remains the most fortified, military confrontation between two enemy forces in the world.

B. Origin of the Korean People

In the most probable theory, the Korean race originated when the Tungustic branch among the Ural-Altaic tribes settled in regions of the Shangtung Peninsula, southern Manchuria and the Korean Peninsula. These people formed one cultural zone in lands around the Yellow Sea with the center at the Gulf of Chihli. Between four and five thousand years ago, the Tungus moved down the Korean Peninsula to settle in the Daedong River Basin near Pyongyang. This makes the Koreans **one of the oldest civilized races in the world**. As people bound by a tight common fate within the confines of a narrow peninsula connected to a vast Asian mainland, Koreans have developed into a homogeneous race with distinctive traits of their own. They speak their own, unique language, **Hangul**, which is a phonetic language containing 10 vowels and 14 consonants and was promulgated by King Sejong the Great and his scholars in 1446.

C. A Brief History of Korea up to the Fourteenth Century

At the dawn of the first century, three kingdoms, all of whom were Buddhist, came into existence throughout the Korean peninsula and the southern part of Manchuria: Goguryo in a part of Manchuria and the northern region of the peninsula, Baekje in the southwestern region of the peninsula and Silla in the southeastern region of the peninsula. Silla unified all three kingdoms in the sixth century with the military help of the Chinese Tang dynasty. However, the unified Silla established her northern boundary as far as modern Pyongyang. In the ninth century, a new kingdom, Goryeo, also Buddhist, replaced the unified kingdom and recaptured the lost northern ground up to the current Korean boundary. The kingdom flourished culturally until it was invaded and conquered by Mongols in 1231. After more than 100 years, the domination of the Mongols was destroyed by the pro-China General Yi Seong Gye, who, in 1392, overthrew Goryeo Kingdom and started the Yi Chosun dynasty based on the Confucian ideology. This kingdom was the last before the modern era. During these first fourteen centuries, the Korean peninsula was repeatedly attacked by northern neighbors, as well as the Mongols. There were numerous civil revolts among the Koreans themselves, but they were able to keep the country together within the peninsula.

D. Korean History for the Last 500 Years

From the beginning of the Yi Chosun dynasty in 1392 to the modern era, the Korean people have both suffered and benefited, voluntarily and

involuntarily, from the interactions with four neighboring countries: China, Japan, Russia (the former USSR) and United States(the US). What follow is the factual presentations of each of these countries' involvement with Korea as they relate to **wars and domination over the Korean peninsula**.

CHINA

The influence of China over the Korean peninsula has been paramount in Korean history. The Chinese Ming dynasty was basically an ally of the Korean Yi Chosun dynasty, which paid tribute to the Chinese. In the seventeenth century, the powerful Manchu dynasty and Ching dynasty in Manchuria attacked the Yi Chosun dynasty. In 1895, China lost the significant Sino-Japanese War to Japan over the Korean issue. And, most recently, during the Korean War, Communist China sent her large army to help the Communist army of North Korea in fighting against the US-backed UN forces which were helping South Korea. In effect, this was a direct military battle between China and the US. This direct conflict ended with the 1953 DMZ truce.

JAPAN

In 1592, Japan made her first attack on the Korean Yi Chosun dynasty with a 150,000-man army. She sent another 140,000 men in 1597. In 1599 at the end of this seven-year war against Korean defenses and the Chinese Ming ally, the Japanese army returned to Japan. In order to become a dominating party on the Korean peninsula, Japan fought and won the Sino-Japanese war in 1895 and the Russo-Japanese war in 1905, ejecting first China and then Russia. Japan then annexed Korea and kept her for 36 years as a colony, an example of Japanese imperialism. On August 15, 1945, Japan, after the US used atomic bombs at Hiroshima and Nagasaki, unconditionally surrendered, ending World War II. And Japan withdrew from Korea.

The history of Japanese oppression of the Korean people during Japan's annexation period is too gruesome and severe for the Korean people to forget easily, even as they might try.

RUSSIA (former USSR)

In 1895 upon Japan's victory in the Sino-Japanese war, Russia sent troops to Seoul in her expansion to the south. This action created friction with Japan, and in 1904, this friction led to the Russo-Japanese war. In the following year, Russia was forced to surrender and signed a peace treaty with Japan. One week before Japan's unconditional surrender on August 15, 1945, the USSR returned to Korea, sending her army into the northern Korean peninsula. This action resulted in the division of postwar Korea into two countries, against the wishes of Korean people. This division brought about the Korean War, which broke out on June 25, 1950. Russia played

a significant role, helping North Korea against the US forces during the Korean War.

UNITED STATES (US)

Regarding the Korean peninsula, US made an important move with the Taft-Katsura Memorandum, which later became significant in terms of the welfare of the Korean people. This memorandum, also called an agreement, was signed by the US Secretary of War, William Howard Taft (who later became the US President), and the Prime Minister of Japan, Katsura Taro, on July 29, 1905. In this agreement, the US recognized Japan's sphere of influence in Korea; in exchange, Japan recognized the US sphere of influence in the Philippines. This secret agreement was not publicized until 1924. It is believed that the Taft-Katsura Agreement violated the earlier Korean-American Treaty of Amity and Commerce signed at Incheon on May 22, 1882, and that it totally disregarded Korean security and sovereignty issues. This agreement can be viewed as the direct cause of Korean colonization by Japan, which inflicted unforgettable misery on the Korean people.

The US began to exert a major, direct influence over the Korean peninsula after the end of WWII. Completely disregarding the wishes of the Korean people, the US, the major victor nation in the Pacific theater, and the USSR agreed to divide Korea between themselves. At the postwar Moscow Conference in December 1945, the two superpowers formed the Joint U.S.-U.S.S.R. Commission which basically ripped Korea into two states along the thirty-eighth parallel, splitting one unique people into two countries. Because of this act, four and a half years later, on June 25, 1950, the Korean War broke out, which in turn brought the Chinese army into the conflict. The military casualties of both sides, as well as the civilian deaths, were incalculable. On July 27, 1953, the conflict ended with the truce that established the DMZ.

Over 50 plus years later the Korean War has still not ended and the unbearable hostility of the two parties continues at the DMZ. At this moment, about 28,000 US army soldiers are still in South Korea. One may question now how many more years will pass until the Koreans see the end of this miserable hostility.

Three conclusions may be drawn from the facts presented concerning the involvement of four powerful nations in Korean affairs. These nations have used the Korean peninsula as a battleground and as an exploitable source in pursuing their own interests in the region. The Koreans have never been strong enough to defend their country or to attack any nation, but have been forced to yield to the demands of others. As a result, these foreign nations have historically inflicted unacceptable misery on the Korean people in the name of humane assistance for them.

Appendix 2

FOUNDERS OF KOREA KINGDOMS OR STATES

There are four well-known founders of new kingdoms or states developed over the Korean peninsula for the last 2000 years. They are Wang Geon of Goryeo, Yi Seong Gye of Yi Chosun Dynasty, Kim Il Sung of North Korea, and Rhee Syng Man of South Korea. The essential features of each founder are compared here in terms of background, mode for rise to power, legacy and family situation. The title of each man designated below is the prefix that person had at the time when he became the head of a new kingdom or state.

A. General Wang Geon (877-943)—Taejo of Goryeo (936-943)

Wang Geon founded Goryeo in 918 and unified the whole Korean peninsula with current northern boundary under Goryeo Dynasty in 936 at his age of 60. He ruled the kingdom until he died in 943.

a. Background
Wang Geon was born in 877 in a wealthy merchant clan based on Songdo (present day Kaesong). His father was Wang Ryung and his mother was Lady Han. His ancestors were known to have lived within ancient Goguryeo boundaries, thus making him a Goguryeo by descent. Wang Geon began his military career in the chaotic Later Three

Kingdoms period. During this period, many local leaders and bandits rebelled against the rule of Silla Queen Jinsung of poor leadership.

b. Rise to Power

   During the chaotic last period of the Unified Silla, there were two powerful rebels developed over Korean peninsula; Gung Ye of northeastern region and Gyeon Hwon of southeastern region. While Gung Ye led his forces into Songdo area in 895, Wang Geon and other local clans surrendered to Gung Ye, and he began his service under Gung Ye's command. In recognition of his military ability, Gung Ye promoted Wang Geon to a general in 900 and appointed him at his age of 37 in 913 as the prime minister of newly renamed Taebong. In 918 when Gung Ye was assassinated due to his harsh ruling, Wang Geon was selected by other generals as a new king of Taebong and renamed the kingdom Goryeo, thus beginning Goryeo Dynasty. In the next year he moved the capital back to his home town, Songdo.

c. Legacy

   The power struggle continued over the peninsula among several factions after Goryeo was founded in 918. In 935, the last king of Silla submitted his kingdom to Goryeo, and in 936, Wang led his forces into Later Baekje area, by bringing his enemies into his ruling coalition. Thus, Wang Geon then made a full-scale unification with agreement of all Korean people over the entire Korean peninsula with its current boundary. He ruled Goryeo until he died in 943.

   The 34th king of Goryeo, Gongyang, was deposed in 1392 by General Yi Seonggye, who ended Goryeo dynasty of 475 years. Gongyang exiled first to Wonju and later to Samchuck where he died.

d. Family

   Wang Geon ruled Goryeo until 943 and had three sons, each becoming a monarch; 2nd monarch Hyejong (943-945), 3rd monarch Jeongjong (946-949) and 4th monarch Gwangjong (949-975).

B. General Yi Seong Gye (Lee Sung-Gye;1335-1408)—Taejo of Chosun(1392-1398) also known as Yi Chosun Dynasty

Yi Seong Gye founded Chosun—Yi Chosun Dynasty in 1392 over the Korean peninsula at his age of 58 and ruled the Dynasty until 1398.

a. Background

Yi Seong Gye was born in 1335 to his father Lee Ja-choon, a former Mongol official with Korean ethnicity, and his mother Lady Choi. His Lee family is believed to be in Cheonju's Lee sector. He joined the Goryeo army and rose through ranks to a general.

During the last years of Goryeo, its foundation was collapsing due to years of war and disintegrating Mongol domination. The kingdom resulted in deep division among various factions. Following the rise of the Ming Dynasty in China, two main groups in the Goryeo court emerged from the various factions: pro-Ming group led by General Yi Seoung Gye and Chong Mong Ju, and pro-Mongol group led by rival General Choi Yeong and Yi Inim.

b. Rise to Power

In 1388 when a Ming messenger came to Goryeo to demand the return of a significant portion of Goryeo's northern territory, General Choi seized the opportunity and played upon the prevailing anti-Ming atmosphere to argue for the invasion of the Chinese Liaodong peninsula. General Yi Seoung Gye was chosen to lead the invasion. At the border of the Yalu River, he made a momentous decision, which would alter the course of Korean history, knowing the domestic and world situation in his favor. He decided to revolt and ordered his men to return back to the capital, Kaesong, to secure the control of the government.

c. Legacy

When General Yi brought his army to the capital, he defeated the forces led by General Choi, who was loyal to the king, and eliminated General Choi. He forcibly dethroned King U in a de facto coup d'etat but did not ascend to the throne right away. For the next four years he enforced his power grasp on the royal court by polarizing himself with new aristocrats. In 1392 one of his 8 sons plotted and executed the plot to kill a pro-Ming, popular Confucian scholar, Chong Mong Ju, who still was loyal to Goryeo King. Then, Yi dethroned the last king, Gongyang, of Goryeo, exiled him to Wonju, and ascended the throne, calling himself the king Taejo of Yi Chosun Dynasty. In 1398 Taejo abdicated during the strife between his sons and died in 1408.

The last king and the second Emperor of Chosun-Yi Dynasty was Soonjong and he was deposed in August 1910 by Japanese colonization of Korean peninsula. Thereby the Yi Chosun Dynasty of 518 years ended.

d. Family

Yi Seoung Gye had 8 sons, 6 from the first wife and the last 2 from the second wife. During the strife between the sons, the 2 sons from the second wife and the second wife were killed. Taejo was succeeded by Jeoungjong, the 2nd son (1399-1400), who was succeeded by Taejong, the 5th son (1400-1418).

C. *General Kim Il Sung (1912-1994)—President of North Korea (DPRK) (1972-1994)*

Kim Il Sung and his followers of the Soviet anti-Japanese army returned to Pyongyang, North Korea from Siberia in September 1945 after the end of WWII when Korea was returned to the Allied forces upon Japan's unconditional surrender. When he arrived in Pyongyang, Kim Il Sung was respected and called General by people of North Korea. He was installed as Prime Minister of North Korea (DPRK) by the Soviets in 1948. He became the President of North Korea in 1972 at his age of 61 according to the newly proclaimed constitution and ruled North Korea basically as a dictator until his death in 1994 at his age of 83.

a.   Background

Kim Il Sung was born into a peasant family in Mangyondae (South Pyongyang), Korea as Kim Song Ju. He was the eldest of 3 sons of Kim Hyong Jik and Lady Kang. In 1920 under Japanese control, his family moved to Manchuria and he attended schools in Jilin.

In 1932 (21 in age), Kim started leading a small group of Korean, anti-Japanese guerrilla group controlled by the Communist party of China. One of famous battles was his guerrilla attack to Japanese force in a province near Mt. Baekdu. During this period, he took the name Kim Il Sung from a former legendary commander who had died. In 1940, Kim's unit reached its peak strength of 300 men and in 1941 he rose to a commander of the unit. During this period of 1935 to 1941, while Kim and many other Korean guerrillas raided Japanese police units, army units and military facilities, many Korean anti-Japanese fighters were killed in battles.

In 1941 (30 in age), when the Japanese drove the anti-Japanese guerrillas from northern China, Kim's group, the only surviving anti-Japanese unit, escaped with his 25 men to a camp near Khabarov, Siberia. After they were investigated by the Soviets, they were pressed into the 88th Special Independence Guerrilla Brigade of the Soviet Army. Kim became Commanding Captain of the Brigade's 1st Battallion

of 200 men. The Brigade continued anti-Japanese activities in the Soviet and Manchuria until the end of WWII in August 1945.

b. Rise to Power

In September 1945 (34 in age), Kim Il Sung and his guerrilla unit of 40 men plus family members returned to Korea with the Soviet forces from Siberia. They arrived at Wonsan, compliment of the Soviet warship Pukachev. Kim was given a hero's welcome at the Pyongyang Municipal Stadium on October 14, 1945. Immediately, he was installed by the Soviets as head of the Provisional People's Committee. He was not, at this time, the head of the Communist Party, whose headquarters were in Seoul in the US occupied South. During his early years as one of Communist Party leaders, he consolidated his power through purges, including assassination and execution of dissident elements within the Party.

By 1948, it was apparent that the immediate unification of Koreans would not be possible. Then, the Soviets responded by appointing Kim (37 in age) Prime Minister of DPRK, as a separate country commonly known as North Korea. In 1949, Kim became the chairman of the Korean Workers Party (KWP).

In December 1972 (61 in age), Kim became President of North Korea according to the new constitution of DPRK just proclaimed. He held this post until his death in 1994.

At the 6th Party Congress in October 1980, Kim publicly designated his son Kim Jong Il as his successor.

c. Legacy

As an anti-Japanese fighter, Kim Il Sung led Communist guerrilla units first in Chinese army and later in Soviet army, until the end of WWII in 1945. His struggle started when he joined a Korean Independence Army in 1930 (19 in age) in Manchuria. During this period of 1930 to 1945, while numerous Korean fighters were killed or captured by the Japanese, Kim managed to survive through the battles against the Japanese. Then he returned to Korea as a hero in September 1945.

Once the Soviet appointed Kim Prime Minister of DPRK in 1948 (37 in age), he established a strong North Korean People's Army with a cadre of guerrillas and former soldiers. On June 25, 1950, he launched a surprise attack on South Korea with the stated intent being the unification of the country under a Communist government. The Korean War began and the war became one of the bloodiest conflicts in world history. It was a civil war as happened many times before in Korean peninsula. However, it brought China and the Soviets into a

direct fight against the United States, as a part of the Cold War between the super powers. More than 1 million soldiers and civilians were killed before the war stopped with a truce at the permanent Armistice Line between North Korea and the US-backed UN on July 27, 1953. Basically, the Korean War continues to this day with enemy hostility without firing at each other.

As the leader of North Korea, Kim ended up switching a Marxist-Leninist ideology to the Juchi (self-reliance) idea and established a personality cult. In this mode, he was referred as "Great Leader" and designated in the constitution as the country's "Eternal President". With his policy and ideology, North Korea became increasingly isolated from the rest of the world. It resulted in an absolute state decorated with socialism, or a dictatorial state which exercises an absolute right to command the people with Workers' Party and Juche ideology in its background. Upon Kim's death in 1994, his presidency of 22 years ended, and his son, Kim Jong Il, succeeded as the second Leader of North Korea.

d. Family
On February 16, 1942 in Siberia, Kim Chong Suk, the second wife of Kim Il Sung, gave birth to their son Kim Jong Il. She joined Kim Il Sung's army in 1935 at her age of 16. She worked as a cook, spy, fighter and wife of Kim Il Sung. She was captured in 1937 by the Japanese and released a year later. She died in 1949.

D. Dr. Rhee Syng Man (1875-1965)—President of South Korea (ROK)(1948-1960)

Dr. Rhee Syng Man returned to Seoul in1945 (71 in age), after the end of WWII when Korea was returned to the Allied forces upon Japan's unconditional surrender. He was chosen as head of a Provisional Government by the US military occupying in the South. He became the President of South Korea in 1948 at his age of 74 by a parliamentary vote, and held the post for 12 years until he was forced to resign by popular 4.19 Student Revolt against a disputed election in 1960. He returned to Hawaii, US where he died in 1965 (91 in age).

a. Background
Rhee was born in 1875 in Whanghai Province, North Korea to Rhee Kyong Sun, a member of an aristocratic family. He soon became active in Korea's struggle against Japanese control. In 1904 (30 in age), he went to the US. He obtained AB degree from George Washington

University and Ph.D. degree from Princeton University in 1910 (36 in age).

In that year, Rhee returned to Korea and found the country was annexed by Japan. His political activities faced unwelcome attention from the occupying Japanese army. In 1912, he gave up his evangelic work in Korea and immigrated to Hawaii as headmaster of a Korean Christian Institute.

On April 8, 1919, the Korean Provisional Government (KPG) was established in the French Concession of Shanghai. The original founders of KPG represented a broad spectrum of the Korean political ideologies united in the common cause of Korean independence and Rhee in absentia was elected president. Unfortunately, the KPG was split into two primary groups; one group seeking militant actions with Soviet backing and Rhee's group favoring diplomatic approach with the US. On December 8, 1920, Rhee entered the KPG office in Shanghai as the president.

As time moved on, the split of the two groups became openly and ugly for the activities of the KPG, leading even to departure or assassination of members. In 1925, Rhee was impeached for embezzlements and returned to Hawaii. Rhee continued his activities for Korea independence with other Koreans in the US until the end of WWII.

b. Rise to Power

In 1945 when Korea was liberated by the Allies forces, Rhee returned to Seoul. The occupying military authority chose Rhee as head of a Provisional Government. With the tacit consent of the authority, Rhee conducted a campaign to remove Communism that was actually a veiled drive to remove all potential opposition and assumed a dictatorial power. In 1948 (74 in age), he was elected the first President of South Korea by a parliamentary vote, defeating Kim Ku who was the last President of Shanghai Korean Provisional Government.

As President, Rhee assumed dictatorial powers with an apparatus of internal security, intimidating Communists as well as opponents, even before the Korean War broke out on June 25, 1960. His government oversaw several massacres, the most notable being on Jeju Island in response to an uprising by leftist faction.

c. Legacy

Rhee had a strong anti-Communist stand throughout his life, which was compatible with the foreign policy of the US. This led to the US choice of Rhee as head of the Korean Provisional Government in the

South Korea at the end of WWII in 1945. He ruled South Korea with iron hands for a period of 15 years, ruthlessly cracking down Communist elements as well as his political opponents. This resulted in countless killings of Koreans.

Rhee faced the breakout of the Korean War on June 25, 1950. During the negotiation for the truce of Korean War, Rhee made a bold order of releasing anti-Communist prisoners-of-war in defiance of major truce negotiators. The fighting between the Communist forces and the western allies stopped with the truce on July 27, 1953 while he was in office.

At the end of his political life, he had to resign in disgrace from his presidency by the student revolt on April 19, 1960, which is a shiny part of Korean history. At the expense of the continuation of divided Korea, current South Korea is economically prosperous as a free and democratic state, far more so than North Korea counterpart as a Communist state. The current, civilian President of South Korea, Mr. Roh, Moo Hyun was elected in a free and democratic election without foreign influence.

d. Family

Rhee married Austrian Francisca Donner on October 8, 1934 (60 in age) in New York City. They adopted a Korean son.

Biographical Record of
Jisoo Ryu, Author

1. PERSONAL

1941. 3 Born at Hamhung, Korea under Japanese control
1945. 6 Family returned to So. Korea when Korea was divided.
1960. 4 Participated 4/19 Student Revolutionary Revolt, Seoul, So. Korea (Toppled Rhee Sygn Man's Government)
1961. 5 Participated 5/16 Military Coup while training at Nonsan, So. Korea (Toppled Chang Myun's Government)
1962. 9 Honorary Discharge from ROK Army, So. Korea (18 mo in service)
1963.12 Departed Korea by US Navy Ship and Arrived at Alameda, CA
1975. 3 Naturalized USA Citizen (Married with 3 grownup children).

2. EDUCATION

1956. 3 Diploma from Daejon Middle School, Daejon, Korea
1959. 3 Diploma from Kyung Bock High School, Seoul, Korea
1963. 12 Attended Seoul National University, Seoul, Korea
1965. 6 B.S. University of Utah, Salt Lake City, Utah
1967. 6 M.S. University of Minnesota, Minneapolis, Minnesota
1971. 8 Ph.D. University of California, Berkeley, California.

3. EXPERIENCES

1973. 4 Assistant Research Professor, University of Utah, S.L.C.
1973. 12 Researcher, UC Space Science Lab., Berkeley.

1977. 8	Research Specialist, Exxon Production Research Co., Houston
1990. 8	Research Associate, Chevron Oil Field Research Co., La Habra.
1993. 2	Associate Professor, King Fahd UPM, Dharan, Saudi Arabia.
1994. 8	Visiting Professor, Seoul National University, Seoul, Korea.
1996. 7	Professor, Gwangju Institute of Science and Technology, Gwangju, Korea (15 mo)
1996.12	Technical Advisor, PEDCO, Seoul, Korea
2005. 6	Retired from professional consultation and Focusing on World Peace, Oakland, CA
2006. 9	Sr. Founding Associate, New World Peace Foundation, Phoenix, AZ.

4. **Miscellaneous**
   — Holding 1 authorship, 10 publications, 11 presentations, and 21 company reports.
   — Member of American Geophysical Union, Washington DC
   — Invited speaker at 1990 3rd Korean Cultural International Conference, Osaka.

Jisoo ("Howard") V. Ryu (유 지 수)
P. O. Box 50563 Phoenix, AZ, 85076 USA
jisooryu@aol.com, jisooryu@gmail.com

www.ingramcontent.com/pod-product-compliance
Lightning Source LLC
Chambersburg PA
CBHW061258280526
45784CB00002B/804